Big
Secrets
to
BUSINESS
SUCCESS

Second Edition

Biblical Secrets to BUSINESS SUCCESS

Second Edition

BOB DIENER

In loving tribute to
my grandfather of blessed memory,

Juda Diener,

who inspired me to succeed
and follow a biblical way of life

and
to my beloved children

Allison, Brianna,
Joshua, Noa, and Seth

Contents

Part 3

Building and Maintaining a Solid Business Reputation

Part 4

Keeping a Biblical Perspective on Wealth and Success

Preface

After graduating from the Cornell Law School in 1982, I went to work for Gibson, Dunn & Crutcher, a huge law firm based in Los Angeles. I spent most of my time drafting documents and advising my clients on the intricacies of the securities regulations. I had no training on how to run a business, but after two years, I decided to follow my real passion of being an entrepreneur full-time. I moved to Hawaii and opened a travel business specializing in airline tickets. I leased space, negotiated supply deals, hired employees, and marketed the business. We were profitable quickly and grew fast. I was constantly confronted with tough questions: how to handle employees, how to handle customers, whether to cut corners or make full disclosures, whether to do deals I wasn't comfortable with for the profit, and more.

I didn't have a mentor. I had no experience. I had no formal business training. But I had the best guidebook to running a successful business ever written – the Bible. When confronted with these questions, I simply followed the biblical principles I had learned for twelve years while studying the Bible in Jewish day school. I went to school at the Hebrew Academy in Miami from first grade until I graduated high school. For those twelve years, I studied Bible, Prophets, Talmud, Proverbs, and more. My guiding light has always been Leviticus chapter 19. Most of what I learned during those twelve years centered on the concepts and principles contained there. I learned the essence of the Bible from the principle of treating others as you want to be treated and from the doctrine of honesty when dealing with others as set forth in Leviticus 19.

Tough dilemmas became easy when viewed from the biblical perspective. I used the Bible as my guide not only for my life outside of business, but also for my business life. I didn't know it then, but looking back now, I realize that this was the secret sauce to my success. As I look at the most successful companies in the world, I realize that they also follow these principles. Companies that cut corners, defraud the public, and operate unethically don't stay in business very long.

Keeping costs low while cheating others will not lead to success. Keeping costs low and treating others fairly is the formula to achieve great success.

I'm a serial conservative entrepreneur. I have founded, run, and sold many businesses. As a conservative entrepreneur, I have always limited risk, kept startup losses to a minimum, and watched the bottom lines closely. I start this book with an outline of the basic principles of conservative entrepreneurship. Although these principals are fundamental to succeeding in business, they only work if combined with biblical principles. Keeping costs low while cheating others will not lead to success. Keeping costs low and treating others fairly is the formula to achieve great success. It is the combination of these two guiding philosophies, I believe, that has been the key to my success, and that's what I'm going to share with you in this book.

After an overview of the principles of entrepreneurship, the book goes through the most important biblical principles that impact running a successful business, such as doing your homework, being honest with customers, paying employees on time, building a solid reputation, and not cutting corners.

Just as important as building a successful business is what to do once you get there. My main motivation in starting my prior businesses was profit. I built solid business infrastructures with fast-growing profit streams, ran the businesses with biblical principles, and then sold the companies. After I sold my last company, hotels.com, I spent several years during my noncompete period thinking about whether I wanted to start up another company. While I love creating unique businesses and earning profits, I also wanted to spend my time helping others and making a difference in this world. Profit was no longer my main motivation, but I still craved the excitement of creating and building a new business.

I decided to become a biblical entrepreneur. A biblical entrepreneur pursues biblical values and charitable giving as the primary goal. Profit is still a goal, but not for its own sake: profit is pursued for the purpose of giving a portion to those in need. Furthermore, profits can only be earned by following the ethical principles in the Bible. All the principles and skills I applied during my career of conservative entrepreneurship were still applicable. I still wanted to make the company profitable and to build a solid, growing business, but not just for personal gain. This time I was aiming much higher. Now I had the motivation to go back into business.

I created my current company, getaroom.com, with these goals in mind. I have all the excitement of creating a new business and making it profitable, but my motivation is using the business as a vehicle for expanding my charitable giving. The more equity and income I transfer to my charitable foundation, the larger my annual pool of funds to donate. The business allows me the opportunity to create programs that raise funds for charity and also enable our employees and customers to become charitable. The business also puts me in a position to meet others in the business world and encourage them to be charitable and run their businesses honestly.

You too can follow these principles and live a more meaningful business life. In this book I will guide you through the process.

Part 1 covers sound biblical and business principles for founding a business that will last. Part 2 explores ways to grow your business within a solid framework of biblical business ideals. Part 3 deals with infusing your business with integrity and honesty, the core of building a successful business.

Part 4 is about how to embody biblical principles in your business once you have reached success. I give examples of things we and other companies have done to operate businesses at a higher level – by giving back. I also show you how to plan for charitable giving when you are ready to sell your business, and how to pass on your values to the next generation. I end with the Talmudic formula for finding the right balance between business, family, personal growth, and community involvement.

The guidelines in this book will help you have a much more meaningful career, live a much more meaningful life, and leave a legacy you can be proud of.

Part 1

Starting Up a Business
Based on Biblical Principles

Work Hard to Succeed

Six days you will labor, and do all your work...
– Exodus 20:8[1]

I have always worked hard. I realized early on that being passive does not work. To be successful in business you need to put in the effort, dedication, and time. I was often able to beat the competition because while they were playing golf or being lazy, I was figuring out ways to get ahead. Many people think that successful people are just naturally successful regardless of the amount of work they do. I don't believe this is true. Successful people have achieved their success because they worked hard at it. They are determined, relentless, and put in the amount of effort necessary to reach their goals. I have always worked long hours and I think about our business all the time.

---

1. There are a small number of verses that are numbered differently in Jewish and Christian Bibles. In Christian Bibles this verse is numbered 20:9.

In my first business, I wired the phone system, answered the phones, and went out almost every night promoting the business. I never looked at the clock, and I still don't. Successful entrepreneurs work long hours, and there is no way around that. Successful entrepreneurs also don't think about the long hours they work because they love what they do and they have the drive and passion to succeed.

> Successful people have achieved their success because they worked hard at it. They are determined, relentless, and put in the amount of effort necessary to reach their goals.

Our Creator put us in this world to be productive members of society. The Bible teaches us that success requires hard work and that we all need to be productive. We already have the tools; the key lies in learning to use our abilities in the most effective way.

We learn in Exodus that we were each given unique talents: "I have filled him with the spirit of God, in wisdom, and in understanding, and in knowledge, and in all manner of workmanship, to devise skillful works, to work in gold, and in silver, and in brass, and in cutting of stones for setting, and in carving of wood, to do all manner of workmanship…and in the hearts of all that are wise-hearted I have put wisdom, that they may make all that I have commanded you" (Exodus 31:3–6). Our Creator gave us the skills and talents we need to succeed, and now it is our obligation to use those skills and talents. No one succeeds by being idle. The Bible condemns laziness: "In all labor there is profit, but the talk of the lips leads only to poverty" (Proverbs 14:23). We need to put in the hard work and time required to succeed.

The Talmud teaches us that it is a great merit to enjoy physical labor and that working hard is key to satisfaction in life. We appreciate what we have when we work hard for it. When I hear complaints about how difficult something is, my response is that you need to go through the hard work to succeed. Furthermore, you will only appreciate the accomplishment after the effort has been put in. To grow intellectually, you need to work hard and diligently in your study. To improve in sports, you need to spend a lot of time in practice. I spend months training for the Half Ironman Triathlon competition every year and have such an amazing feeling of accomplishment when I cross the finish line. I would never be able to complete the race without the months of hard work and training. Getting up at 5 AM and training for two or three hours a day is a lot of work but it pays off.

"Greater is one who enjoys physical labor than one who is pious and idle" (Babylonian Talmud, *Berachot* 8a). The same is true in business. It takes hard work to bring success and fulfillment. Psalms teaches us that enjoying the fruits of your labor brings great contentment: "Happy are those who fear God, [but] when you enjoy the labor of your hands, you shall be happy and it will be well with you" (Psalms 128:1–2). That's why it is so exciting to be an entrepreneur – there is so much satisfaction from your hard work of creating a business and watching it grow and blossom. You appreciate everything you have so much more when you know you have earned it honestly by the labor of your own hands.

Don't view your work as a nine-to-five job. While you are at work, work hard. "One who is slack in his work is a brother to him who destroys" (Proverbs 18:9). Work hard and be diligent and passionate about your work – this is the road to success. Proverbs continues: "He who tills his ground will have plenty of bread, but he who follows worthless pursuits lacks sense" (Proverbs 12:11). Untended gardens don't bear fruit. Likewise, successful entrepreneurs work hard and put a lot of energy into planning, creating, maintaining, and growing their businesses.

You also need employees who feel invested in your business and aren't just marking time until they can punch out and go home. I believe in creating incentives for sales employees. Look for sales employees who are more interested in the incentives than in the base salary. This shows that they are willing to work hard and that they believe in themselves. Every employee in our company has an ownership interest in the company through stock option grants. This creates the right incentives for employees to work hard to build up the business of which they are part owners. In our prior companies, many employees earned more through their stock options than they did with their base salary. We want employees who appreciate the value of owning equity and want to work hard for it.

Similar principles apply to encouraging the next generation to be productive members of society. We learn from the Bible that just supporting our children without teaching them how to stand on their own feet is a big mistake. It states in the Talmud that "One who does not teach a child a trade is as though the child were taught to be a robber" (Babylonian Talmud, *Kiddushin* 29a). I believe it is important to find the right balance between financial support for the next generation and creating an environment where they have the passion and incentives to work hard in pursuing a career. Encourage growth through continued education and work experience rather than enabling people in a dependent lifestyle. They will appreciate you much more when you teach them the value of hard work and give them the tools to become self-sufficient. The rewards of financial gain are so much greater when you understand the hard work involved to get there.

Ten Questions to Ask Yourself before You Start Up Your Business

1. Am I ready to work hard? . . . . ✓

2. Am I ready to make sacrifices for work? . . . . ☐

3. What hours am I comfortable working? _____

4. Have I discussed the commitment required with
   my spouse/significant other and family? . . . . ☐

5. Can I overcome the frustration of temporary
   failure for the sake of long-term success? . . . . ☐

6. How will I handle things taking longer
   and being harder than expected? _____

7. Am I willing to think about my business all the time? . . ☐

8. Am I a roll-up-the-sleeves type of person? . . . . ☐

9. Can I achieve a balance of work,
   family, and social commitments? . . . . ☐

10. Do I know when to take a breather so I don't burn out? . . ☐

Do Your Homework

He who deals with a slack hand becomes poor,
but the hand of the diligent makes rich.
– Proverbs 10:4

I learned the principle of due diligence through Talmudic study. For years, I studied debates among rabbinical scholars on various topics. Nothing was taken for granted – all arguments were considered and debated. Issues were thoroughly vetted. I learned to ask *why* and to make sure I understood the issues. Studying alone was not enough: we were paired with other students and spent much of our time discussing the issues with our study partners. We learned to tear each other's arguments apart. We read every commentary on the topic we could find.

I approached business the same way. I did my homework. I researched the competition. I tested the market. I argued the other side. There is no shortcut for doing your homework in a business and understanding the competitive landscape. Major mistakes can often be avoided and opportunities found by speaking to experts and analysts, tearing apart business plans, doing market studies and focus groups, analyzing expenses, and doing your homework – due diligence.

There is no shortcut for doing your homework in a business and understanding the competitive landscape.

I'm constantly contacted by entrepreneurs who are convinced they have the best business plan ever put together, and when I ask them how they are going to make a profit, I often get a blank stare. Many tell me they will sell ads on their website. When I ask them how they are going to get customers to the website, they usually tell me they will buy keywords on Google. It all sounds great until we get into the details. I ask them if they have investigated the cost of buying Google ads and what their expected ROI will be. Many don't know what ROI is. (It's return on investment.) They don't know what the Google ads will cost. They also have no idea what percentage of customers will click their ads or what the look-to-book ratio will be – that is, the number of clicks they will pay for as opposed to the number of customers who actually will purchase the product. When I ask them how they are going to start a business when they don't even know if they can run the business profitably, I often get another blank stare.

When we start to discuss the profit potential of selling ads, I ask if they know how much they can sell the ads for and who is going to buy them. I ask them why anyone would buy ads on their site if they have no traffic. Blank stares. Almost no one realizes that it will be difficult to excite much interest in buying ads on a website that has – at least initially – limited traffic. And they all think their ad space is worth ten to one hundred times more than they are likely to actually get for the ads – assuming they can find buyers at all. Blank stares again.

They usually want to market their product globally and when I tell them it will cost them $10 million a month to do what they want to do, I get even more blank stares.

This is the kind of talk I often hear from those who approach me with a business plan. They haven't done their due diligence. The right way is to diligently study, prepare, debate, and come up with a business plan that is well thought out.

Before we launched getaroom.com, we spent months studying the market. We knew the business models of all the competition, conducted many focus groups to understand the market, and developed new business models that had not been done before. We tested the waters slowly and conservatively until we figured out what worked. We spoke extensively with almost every industry expert to get the perspective of the pros. In short, we did our homework.

Take your time and prepare. Follow the advice of Proverbs 21:5: "The thoughts of the diligent lead only to abundance, but everyone who is hasty comes only to want." Don't be in a rush to conquer the world. Unless you have the pocketbook of a company like Microsoft, you will most likely need to start your business slowly and carefully. Figure out what works first, and then you can expand. Understand the market so you don't waste valuable funds on a business that was not thought out well.

In short, do your homework.

Ten Musts for Due Diligence

Here are a few critical items to think about
as part of your due diligence process.

1. Who are the competitors and what is their business model?

2. Are there any public companies in the space and have I read their public filings cover to cover?

3. Do I have financial projections, and have I asked an unbiased accountant to tear them apart?

4. How am I going to bring customers in?

5. What is my cost of acquiring customers?

6. What is my value proposition (the value I will offer to my customer)?

7. How am I different from the competition and why will customers use my service over others?

8. How much risk do I need to take and how do I limit the risk?

9. Are there any research firms covering this industry and have I read their publications and talked to them?

10. Do I have the skills to run this business?

Use Your Talents
to Find the Right Business

He has filled them with wisdom of heart to do all
manner of workmanship, of the craftsman, and of
the skillful workman, and of the weaver in colors, in
blue, and in purple, in scarlet, and in fine linen, and
of the weaver, and of anyone who does professional
work and designs skillfully.

– Exodus 35:35

According to Kabbalah, each of us comes into this
world with a unique mission. Our family, social,
and business lives are all tools given to us to fulfill
our mission. No two people come into this world
with the same calling. We are all given a light to shine upon
this world and tasked with making it a better place than when

we arrived through the use of these tools. We were each given unique talents. It is up to each of us to discover our unique mission based upon the tools we were given.

You can use your business, profession, or work as a platform to fulfill your mission. A business, a job, a career is a tool to create wealth to help make the world around us better, by donating part of that wealth to those in need or by using the tools of our work lives to help others.

In selecting the business that is right for you, think about your unique talents and how you can use those talents to create something new and different that can create value for others. First identify your talents, then find a business where you can best use those talents to be profitable. Finally, use part of those profits to improve your community. You need to be passionate about your business. You need to build something that is better than what is out there now.

Perhaps you have great speaking ability, great motivational ability, great teaching ability, great organizational skills, great analytical skills, or great management skills. Perhaps you can draw, sing, dance, or compose music or beautiful poetry. Perhaps you have an uncanny ability to digest, summarize, and present information clearly. Perhaps you are a compassionate listener or a born leader. Whatever your unique talents and skills are, know that they have been given to you to fulfill your mission. When you build a business that utilizes these talents most effectively, operate your business in a biblically ethical way, and help others

> In selecting the business that is right for you, think about your unique talents and how you can use those talents to create something new and different that can create value for others.

through your business and talents, you will feel great inner happiness.

There is no greater pleasure in life than fulfilling your mission. When you realize your purpose in life and use your business as a platform to get there, you reach a high level of spiritual fulfillment. You also will maintain a high level of enthusiasm for and excitement about your business.

Ever since I was young I have loved travel and technology. My dad traveled all over the world and I was always excited about the stories and adventures he told us. During college summers, I traveled through Europe and the Middle East. When I completed law school, I traveled all over the world. I also loved technology and wanted the first version of any new device. I had the first model laptop computer, the first model fax machine and the first model cell phone.

I also loved business. I started my business career at seven years old. I had a booth in front of our house selling cookies and fruit punch. I bought the fruit punch concentrate at the food store for five cents and sold drinks for ten cents each. Each pack made a big pitcher, which served about fifteen drinks. So I earned $1.50 from every drink package I bought for five cents, or thirty times my cost. Not a bad profit. I baked the cookies with my mom and sold them also for a nice profit. I was so excited to make money and then used the profits to buy toys and candy.

When I was fourteen, I started helping my dad in his tile and marble business. I saw an advertisement from the *Miami Herald* that they were offering a special deal for placing ads in the Sunday newspaper. I designed an ad and placed it in the newspaper when no one else in the business was advertising. The business boomed from the ads. I suggested to my dad that he open the showroom on Sundays when everyone else in the business was closed, because many people don't have time to shop during the week. My dad was skeptical about whether anyone would come in on Sunday, but the parking lot was full all day long. We were filling orders as fast as we could write them down.

I was way ahead in math and took advantage of the classified ad deal for students: ten dollars for four lines. I advertised my services as a math tutor and soon had a full roster of students. I tutored math to other kids in the community – even those much older than me – and made a lot of money. When I turned sixteen and learned how to drive, I bought my first car for $600, a 1966 light blue Mustang. When it broke and I had no money to fix it, I went to auto mechanics school and learned how to fix cars. I then bought cars, repaired them, and sold them for a nice profit. Our driveway was always filled with cars.

After the first year in law school, I had more time and was determined to figure out a way to make money. When I was traveling around the country interviewing with law firms, one of the airlines was giving out vouchers for 50 percent off the next flight. Most passengers threw them in the garbage. I figured they must be worth something so I cleaned out every garbage can I could find. I went to other airports and did the same thing. I contacted some travel agencies in New York to see if they were interested in buying the coupons and realized these were very valuable. I kept going to airports and cleaning out the garbage cans, and then headed to New York to sell the vouchers. It was a great part-time business for a law school student.

Then my cousin came to visit and told me about the new frequent flyer programs. The airlines were now not only giving out 50 percent off vouchers but free tickets. I figured these must really be valuable. I started buying these for $100 and selling them for $300. I put small classified ads in newspapers offering to buy and sell these, and presto, my part-time business in law school was booming. I continued this on the side while practicing law until it grew into a bigger business and I had to decide between law practice and the airline business. I decided to leave law practice and pursue my passion for travel, business, and technology.

My law school classmate and friend Dave Litman and I started a business that created a secondary market to exchange these tickets. Airlines were also giving out free, transferable tickets to customers who were bumped from flights, and offering tickets in trade for merchandise. The weaker airlines such as World Airways, Pan Am, and Eastern were getting more aggressive with giving out free tickets. Our business grew. As the weaker airlines went out of business or were taken over by the stronger carriers, the surviving airlines started to place more restrictions on transferability. We decided it was time to sell the business and move on. The timing was good, as shortly thereafter the Gulf War broke out and travel came almost to a standstill.

After sitting around the beach for a few months, we were bored and started looking for our next business. My partner Dave had great skills at management and organization, and a talent for handling employees and technology. My skills were sales, finance, public relations, and marketing. We decided that whatever we did, we would each focus on the talents and skills that we had. We looked for a business with a large market, with limited downside risk (the financial risk of potential losses that could be incurred) but almost unlimited upside potential (the conceivable return on investment), no inventory, no storefront locations needed, and where we could create great values.

We didn't want to risk any of the funds we had earned and saved from the last business. We didn't think we could get a loan and didn't want to ask family for money. We didn't want to go to friends for funds and risk hurting the friendships. We therefore needed a business we could start with no or minimal up-front investment. We already knew the travel business and how to market to consumers and travel agents.

We also did our research, investigating publicly available information on the travel industry in research company publications and from organizations such as the American Hotel and Motel Association. We knew our stuff – we just had to decide how exactly to turn our knowledge, passion, and skills into a profitable business that would contribute something valuable to the market.

After a few days of scuba diving and living in a hut in Belize, Dave and I had analyzed our options. We decided to go into the hotel business and create a market for excess hotel rooms. Hotel occupancy was only about 60 percent, and hotels needed close to 70 percent occupancy on average just to break even. They needed new sources of distribution. We believed our skills would best be utilized in this business.

It was also a very fragmented market, leaving us room to maneuver. There are over fifty thousand hotels in the US alone. World-class cities such as Paris have over four thousand hotels. This large number of hotels, most of which were independent or franchised, created a great competition to fill empty rooms. We were not beholden to a handful of vendors that controlled the inventory. We didn't have to do business with every hotel – we just needed enough great deals in top destinations to have a great business. The airline, car rental, and cruise businesses all had a small number of vendors that had most of the inventory and so those were much more difficult businesses in which to achieve success. In those industries, we would have had to work with all of the vendors to have a viable business, regardless of the consumer value.

Hotels had rooms they could not sell and the rooms were what we call in our business a "perishable" commodity. An empty hotel room is a valuable commodity late in the day, but by the time the wee hours of the morning roll around, it's worthless. The hotel has spent money on furnishing and maintaining the room, and it has earned nothing for its investment, like a grocer who watches his ripe tomatoes turn rotten on his shelves. If we could bring the hotels customers for those rooms that they could not find on their own, it was a win-win: not only did the hotels add to their sales and profits, but we earned a commission and travelers had access to better deals.

Travelers were very frustrated in booking hotels in those days, because there was no central source to find rates and rooms other than travel agencies, which typically did not want to book hotels. Calling a chain was helpful only for that chain's hotels but not for any others, so it took many phone calls to shop rates or find availability during busy periods.

Travel agents didn't have it that much easier than consumers. Many hotels were not connected to the systems travel agents used, so the travel agent had to get on the phone and call hotels one by one just like the customer would have had to do. Furthermore, hotels paid commission only after the customer's stay, not at the time of booking, so agents had to wait months to receive commissions from hotel bookings. Many hotels found excuses not to pay the commission at all, and it usually was not worth the agents' time to chase after their rather small commission from recalcitrant hotels. Instead they just avoided booking hotels altogether and focused on airline tickets, from which they received a nice profit, with their commission paid up front. It is very different today, but those were the market dynamics at the time.

We wanted to create an efficient marketplace for hotels to sell their excess rooms and for travelers to find deals. This was 1991 and there was no Internet at the time. There were many independent hotels that could not afford to regularly take out ads to offer their hotel rooms. And in any event there usually wasn't enough time to advertise rooms for the next day that were going unsold.

Dave and I looked closely at the hotel industry, analyzed the market dynamics, saw the needs of the hotel owners and travelers, and we founded a business that used our talents. We found a way to create value for both our suppliers and our customers. We created the Hotel Reservations Network, a central marketplace for hotel rooms through the use of a toll-free phone number. Now hotels could move unsold rooms, and consumers had one central phone number to call for deals.

The business met all the right criteria for us. There was minimal up-front investment required, as we did not need storefronts and there was no inventory for us to transport and store. To keep initial costs low, we held off on hiring employees at first and did everything ourselves. I negotiated special rates with hotels. Dave handled the computer programming, customer service, and fulfillment. We both answered the phone booking reservations.

At first, we worked on a commissionable model from hotels, but many hotels did not pay us the commission owed. We were spending most of our time acting as a collection agency trying to collect our commissions and realized this model was not going to work. There was poor cash flow and it was going to require more up-front investment. We had invested $1200 so far – $600 each – and did not want to invest more. We then came up with a great idea: Why not have our customers pay us up front for the hotel rooms? We would collect directly from the customers and negotiate credit terms with the hotels so we could pay them thirty days after checkout. We called this the "merchant model." If we could pull this off, we never would have cash flow issues.

There was only one problem: What hotel would give us terms? That is, who would extend credit to us? We were a new business with no track record. No hotel would give us credit, but we were not ready to give up. We started with one hotel where we were booking a lot of reservations in New York. We basically pleaded for terms and promised to pay weekly. After making our payments on time for several weeks, we asked the hotel if they would act as a reference for other hotels. We soon had tens and then hundreds of hotels with credit. We now had great cash flow as our customers paid us up front for hotels and we typically had thirty days to pay the hotels after they billed us.

We now had a good flow of funds to expand our business and did not need to invest any up-front funds. We created great value for our hotels by bringing them a new market of consumers for their rooms, and great value for consumers by getting them better rates and an easy marketplace to find deals. This model had limited downside and almost unlimited upside.

In 1995 things really took off when we discovered the Internet and built our first website. This company later became the world's largest online hotel booking company, hotels.com.

Dave and I both used our talents to start and build this business. I used my negotiating, business, legal, marketing, and finance skills to negotiate with hotels, set up the finance and accounting systems, do the legal work, and market the company. Dave used his employee relations, computer programming, and organizational skills to build the infrastructure, technology, call centers, and operational part of the business. We turned the company into our vehicle for charitable giving. Every time we had a liquidity event by selling a portion of our ownership in the company, we put a portion of the proceeds into our foundations. We used and continue to use our foundations to fund many charities that we believe are making a great difference.

Is It Right for Me?

Here are a few things to ask yourself
when searching for the business
that will maximize your potential.

1. What are my talents?
2. What are my weaknesses?
3. What do I enjoy?
4. What am I passionate about?
5. How am I better suited to do this than others before me?
6. How much risk am I comfortable taking?
7. How much capital will I need?
8. How much capital will I put in?
9. How much capital will I have access to?
10. What is my goal for the business?
11. What is my upside?
12. How large is the industry?
13. Do I have strong motivational skills?
14. How strong are my analytical skills?
15. How strong are my sales skills?
16. Who am I comfortable selling to?
17. Do I prefer to work alone or with partner(s)?
18. What hours will I need to work?
19. Am I ready for a lifestyle change?
20. Will I put in the hours and effort necessary?

Determine Your Value Proposition

Why is this night different?
– Passover Haggadah

On Passover the youngest child asks at the beginning of the Seder: "Why is this night different from all other nights?" The Passover Haggadah then tells the story of why this night is different. You need to ask yourself the same question about your business: How is it different from all other competitive businesses? What unique value are you bringing to the marketplace? When we created hotels.com, we created a new way to book hotels on the Internet and offered lower prices and a simple way to book hotels. This was a great value proposition: we had great value to offer to our customers – value they could not get elsewhere.

The first question I usually get asked about getaroom.com is how it is different from hotels.com and the other online travel agents, many of which have excellent product, huge marketing budgets, and good management. This is also the main question I asked myself before going back into the online hotel business. We decided not to compete head-on with the other OTAs (online travel agents) but to focus on segments of the market that were left untouched. We created two new ways to book hotels and get special value with getaroom.com. First, we created the Unpublished Rate program, where we contract with hotels for lower rates that are only available through our call center. Consumers who call us get lower rates at participating hotels in our call center than anywhere online. These rates are typically 10–20 percent less than the lowest online rate but can be as much as 60 percent less. To convince hotels to participate in this program, we kept the pricing opaque.

When consumers call us, we tell them the lowest online rate and that we have a less expensive Unpublished Rate that is exclusively available in our center. We don't tell them the rate, but give them the range of typical savings. We tell them that typically the Unpublished Rate is 10–20 percent off the online rate. After they give us their credit card details and commit to the booking, we reveal the rate, which can often be much more than 10–20 percent off – even as high as 60 percent off. This way, consumers know they are getting a lower rate than what they saw online but they just don't know the exact rate. The purpose of keeping the rate opaque is to avoid competing with the hotel's distribution channels. This is the condition the hotels have for allowing us to offer such attractive savings. There may be cancellation penalties for canceling the lower Unpublished Rate that don't apply when booking the higher rate. The Unpublished Rate program is not for everyone, but savvy consumers who are willing to spend a few minutes on the phone can save a lot of money. Hotels benefit as well because they move rooms that would otherwise go unsold.

There are other opaque ways to book in the marketplace, such as when the pricing is revealed but the hotel name is kept secret or opaque. The consumer specifies the star rating and area of a destination they want to be in, but they don't know the hotel name. Although the pricing is usually excellent, we found that this opaque program only attracts a limited percentage of the marketplace since most people want to know exactly where they will be staying before committing to a booking. By disclosing the hotel name but not the price, we put consumers at ease, and they feel more comfortable proceeding with the booking.

Many consumers are less reluctant to rent cars or book airlines in this opaque system since there are only a few providers and they are very similar. It is very different with hotels because almost every hotel is unique. You also spend a lot more time in your hotel room than in a car or on an airplane. With those other opaque systems, if you are not happy once you hear the hotel name and location, you are stuck, as they are usually nonrefundable.

We thus created a system that gives consumers an alternative way to find a hotel deal and removes the concern about ending up with a hotel they don't want. Our Unpublished Rate program gives customers the hotel name; they just don't know the exact price. But they know they are going to get a better deal than they can find anywhere else and they have an approximate idea of the savings. If they need to cancel, there may be a $25 penalty, but they are not stuck. The cancel rate for our Unpublished Rates is a fraction of the average industry cancel rate, because the reason most people cancel is that they found a better deal somewhere else. Since our deal is lower than the market rate to begin with, very few people cancel.

Second, we created a Flash Sale system where hotels push special pricing – lower than they offer anywhere else – with the catch that it must be booked within a short time window. Consumers usually have anywhere from two to twenty-four hours to book the special rate and can stay anytime. To find these, customers simply go to getaroom.com, enter their destination and travel dates and the Flash Sales will have either clocks showing how much time is left on the sale, or they will see the price slashed out, with the special Flash Sale pricing and a notation about how much time is left to book. We offer these almost daily in major markets worldwide.

We know from surveys that most consumers don't make an immediate decision about their hotel stay. They come back to the site an average of three or four times before making a decision and usually take a few days to commit. They keep shopping in the hopes of finding a better deal. We created this program to shorten the decision period and keep customers on our site by offering a compelling reason to book now. The consumer is rewarded for the quick decision by saving 5–60 percent off the lowest online price. The same terms of cancellation typically apply whether or not there is a Flash Sale. If the hotel is cancelable up to day of check-in with no penalty, then the same cancellation policy generally applies to the Flash Sale.

Although bookings must be completed within the time specified for the special rate, dates of stay are usually not limited. The hotel thus books a lot of rooms in a short period of time and the consumer gets a great deal. Although the pricing is lower than the rate the hotel or other online sites offer to the public, it is for such a short period of time that the hotels don't view these deals as competitive. They are unique, very short-term promotions that are only available when booked immediately. Once the Flash Sale period is over, the special can no longer be booked.

Our Unpublished Rate program and Flash Sales are two great value propositions we created with getaroom.com. We also built a great call center that gives us a big competitive advantage because almost all of our competitors outsource their call centers overseas. Most other online travel companies don't like the call center. They view it as an unwanted expense and work hard to push the online traffic. Some have long hold times and the level of customer service may not be the greatest. By building a local US-only call center with highly trained and knowledgeable agents, and offering quick answer times and a very high level of customer service, we found an area of the market that was mostly abandoned and that represented a wide-open opportunity.

Many consumers still want to book with a knowledgeable agent and get suggestions on which hotel to book. Even in a fully automated transaction, consumers are more comfortable booking with us, because they know we are available 24/7 to assist them if there is ever an issue with their booking. We have built up a loyal clientele by having this competitive advantage in a marketplace that traditionally has very little customer loyalty. We believe that the online experience needs to be a blend of on- and offline and that strong offline support is critical to long-term success.

By focusing on the call center, we are also able to offer the Unpublished Rate system and present better deals to consumers. Although the call center is more expensive to operate than the online site, we figured out great efficiencies in the call center that keep call times low and service levels high. We refer consumers back to the online site when appropriate. We help consumers make a quick decision. Most consumers already know the hotel or narrow range of hotels they want before they call, and they simply don't have online access when they are calling or just want to book the Unpublished Rate.

As mobile usage for hotel bookings continues to grow, our competitive advantage in the call center is even more important, as mobile users tend to call more. Our talk times are a fraction of industry averages and our close ratios are much higher than industry averages. Some of our phone numbers close bookings at rates as high as 80 percent. We have figured out ways to operate a very efficient call center through our long-term expertise, great management, and best practices, while our competition has shied away from this. This has enabled us to be the leader in this area.

We figured out new ways to get consumers better rates and values with getaroom.com. We found and continue to find special niches in the marketplace where we don't have competition. What are you going to offer your customers? Make sure you can answer this first fundamental question of what your value proposition is before going further in your business. It is very difficult to lure customers to a new company that they never heard of before. When you are out competing with big-brand names and established companies that have been in the business for a long time, you need to offer people a compelling reason to choose your service over others.

What are you going to offer your customers? You need to offer people a compelling reason to choose your service over others.

There are many ways to create value as we did at getaroom.com, such as better pricing, better service, ease of use, solving problems, creating efficiencies, and more. At the end of the day, your business is all about value. Your customers use you because you present a unique value to them. Your employees work for you because you offer value – potentially valuable equity, good benefits, a great atmosphere, a challenging and rewarding environment, and more. Your partners work with you because you offer them something they can't get elsewhere.

Flesh out your value proposition so you can easily articulate it. Create focus groups and listen to what consumers tell you about your value proposition. Is it good enough to convince a consumer to use your company instead of a company they have been using for years?

Ask if consumers believe your value proposition. So many companies advertise up to 50 percent off – or even more – that few consumers believe these claims. You must do more to prove your value proposition so that consumers believe you. There are lots of effective ways to do this, but few new companies do it right. One effective way is to use testimonials. On getaroom.com, we have a link to tons of testimonials from our customers regarding the great values and service they received. I'm always amazed at how many people read these testimonials as well as the hotel reviews we place on the site. Consumers want to read other consumers' opinions. One of the main reasons consumers use our service is because they were referred to us or read a positive story or testimonial about us. Travelers tend to book hotels that others raved about. This is one of the most effective ways to prove your value proposition: show how others have successfully used your company.

Be clear about your value proposition. Your customers need to understand why they should use your company instead of the competition. When you have a real value proposition and clearly articulate it, consumers will flock to your company.

What Is My Value Proposition?

☞ How is my product different from the competition?

☞ What does the consumer gain by using my product over others?

☞ Can I articulate my value proposition in a few short words?

☞ As a consumer, would I buy my product?

☞ Have I asked others if they believe in my value?

☞ Have I researched all of the competition?

Hire – and Keep –
the Right Employees

The little you had before I came
has increased abundantly.
– Genesis 30:30

H iring the right employees and treating them right is key to success. I have seen this blessing come to fruition in each of my businesses. We learn about the value of finding the right employees and how much an employee can improve your business from the famous biblical story of Jacob and Laban. Jacob went to work for Laban, his future father-in-law, in exchange for marrying his daughter. The term was seven years. When the time was up and Jacob was to marry his intended after all those years of hard labor, Laban tricked Jacob by giving him the older daughter, Leah, instead of Rachel. Jacob ended up working another seven years for Rachel.

During his employment, he was loyal and Laban grew wealthy. "You know how I have served you," Jacob said to Laban when he was ready to leave, "and how your cattle have fared with me. The little you had before I came has increased abundantly, and the Lord has blessed you wherever I turned" (Genesis 30:29–30).

Jacob continues in the next chapter: "These twenty years that I have been with you, your ewes and your she-goats have not miscarried their young, and I have not eaten the rams of your flocks. That which was torn of beasts I did not bring to you; I bore the loss of it.… In the day, scorching heat consumed me, and the frost by night, and my sleep fled from my eyes" (Genesis 31:38–40). Jacob was honest, devoted, and hardworking. God blessed Laban because Jacob was working for him. Because Laban found a great employee, he reaped great success.

Your task as an entrepreneur is to find the right people and then motivate them to perform at their best. I have learned over and over through various companies that trying to grow the company with the wrong employees does not work. The worst position to be in is when you have a decent employee who is just not good enough to get your company to the next level, an employee who is a B player when you need an A player. When someone is not top notch but not bad enough to fire, you are in a terrible situation that could even prove to be the downfall of your company. You have an obligation to that employee and to yourself to let such a person go, or at least to find a more appropriate position for him or her within your company. You will never get your company to the next level when you have mediocre people in key positions.

This is often one of the toughest decisions to make in a growing company. You may have an employee who has been with the company for a long time and is trying hard but is just in over his or her head. You don't feel comfortable firing this person but you also know he or she can't do the job. The best way to handle this is to be honest and fair. Discuss the situation with the employee. Offer a more suitable position within your company or help to secure a more suit-able position somewhere else. Be fair and generous with your severance package and your now-former employee will ap-preciate what you have done. If you drag it out, however, and allow a bad situation to continue, both you and your employee will be frustrated. The longer you wait, the longer it will take to get to the level you want to get to.

> Your task as an entrepreneur is to find the right people and then motivate them to perform at their best.

You also need to treat your employ-ees fairly. We learn this from Leviticus. "The wages of a worker shall not remain with you all night until the morning" (Leviticus 19:13). One of the most difficult parts of running a business is dealing with employee issues. Employees can be demanding. They will want raises and time off; there will be expenses and conflicts and more. When confronted with these issues, I just think about the principal of paying employees on time that I learned from Leviticus. As long as you treat your employees fairly and honestly, they will respect you and your decisions.

We are also commanded in Deuteronomy chapter 24 not to take advantage of employees: "You shall not abuse a poor and needy laborer, whether a fellow countryman or a stranger.... You shall pay him his wages on the same day – nor shall the sun go down first, for he is poor and urgently depends on it – lest he cry to the Lord against you and you will incur guilt" (Deuteronomy 24:14–15). This taught me to always treat employees equally and fairly. I have always applied an absolute level of fairness among all our employees when it comes to pay and all other issues. Race, age, gender, religion, color – these have no bearing. It is always difficult to say no, but often necessary. When you develop a reputation for fairness to your employees, they respect you more and know that they were treated properly.

We learn from the Bible to pay our bills on time and pay contractors on time. Many people live from paycheck to paycheck. If you do not pay in a timely fashion, you may be putting them at undue hardship. The Talmud stresses how important it is to pay workers on time: "For he is poor and urgently depends on it – Why did this worker climb the ladder, suspend himself from a tree, and risk death? Was it not for his wages?" (Babylonian Talmud, *Bava Metzia* 112a).

The Bible also teaches that employees have an obligation to their employers to put in a full day's work and be productive. The *Mishneh Torah*, a compilation of biblical law, states: "Just as the employer is enjoined not to deprive the poor worker of his hire or withhold it from him when it is due, so is the worker enjoined not to deprive the employer of the benefit of his work by frittering away his time, a little here and a little there, thus wasting the whole day deceitfully. Indeed, the worker must be very punctilious in the matter of time" (*Mishneh Torah*, Laws of Hiring 13:7). Billing a client for more hours than you worked or not working the time you are paid for is the same as theft. "Just as theft of money is theft, so is theft of time" (*The Path of the Just* 11).

Employers who deal fairly with their employees also motivate them to give their all and to honestly and loyally fulfill their side of the employer-employee relationship. Treat your employees well, pay them on time, and you will earn their trust and loyalty. They will feel more comfortable in their work environment and they will work harder. This is the way to build your business – by keeping your employees motivated and loyal.

Top Ten Things to Consider before Hiring

1. How much interest does the applicant show in the business?
2. Why does he or she want to work for me?
3. Did the candidate do sufficient homework to learn about my business?
4. Is he or she passionate about working for my company?
5. What was the reason for leaving his or her former employment?
6. Is this a long-term employee? How often has this person switched positions and why? Where does he or she want to be in five years?
7. Did the applicant ask the right questions?
8. Did he or she care more about the opportunity or the benefits?
9. Does this person fit in with our environment?
10. Is this a hard and dedicated worker?

Part 2

Using Biblical Principles to Grow Your Business

Limit Risk

Do not be among those who shake hands, or who go into debt; if you are not able to pay, why should [the creditor] take away your bed from under you?
– Proverbs 22:26

nlike investing, where as you increase risk you increase return, in a business increasing risk does not equate to higher returns. It is your task as an entrepreneur to limit your risk. This is not to say you have to be timid: you can keep risk to a minimum and still have large upside. But you need to understand the risk in your business and work to tame it. The Bible teaches us to limit risk and to be prudent. Proverbs 22:26 states: "Do not be among those who shake hands, or go into debt; if you are not able to pay, why should [the creditor] take away your bed from under you?" In other words, do not take excessive risk and leave yourself in a position to lose everything.

The Bible also teaches us to limit risk when investing funds. It teaches us the principle of asset allocation, or not putting all your eggs in one basket. Ecclesiastes 11:2 teaches us: "Divide a portion into seven and even into eight, for you do not know what bad thing will happen on earth." The principle of asset allocation is expounded in the Babylonian Talmud, written more than fifteen hundred years ago: "Let every man divide his money into three parts, and invest a third in land, a third in business, and a third let him keep by him in reserve" (*Bava Metzia* 42a). We should apply these principles of risk management when running our businesses. Here are seven tips to help you learn how to build your business with an appropriate level of risk.

> Unlike investing, where as you increase risk you increase return, in a business increasing risk does not equate to higher returns.

1. Limit your investment.

One of the first pieces of advice I give to people starting a business is to start small and limit the amount of investment. Most entrepreneurs have grand plans that require large up-front investments. Starting this way usually leads to failure. It is a much better strategy to start small and not put a large amount of investment capital at risk. Watch your bottom line closely and only spend when you have to spend so you don't take on more investment funds than you really need.

If you borrow money from others, you need to treat it as your own money. As Ethics of the Fathers cautions, "Let your friend's property be as precious to you as your own" (Ethics of the Fathers 2:16). If you raise venture funds from others, treat those funds the same as if they were your own dollars. Treating raised capital more liberally than your own capital is a poor way to run a business and often results in wasting money.

You tend to lose discipline when you have too much available capital, especially when you borrowed it from others. The Bible teaches us that there should be no difference in the way you treat borrowed funds from the way you would treat your own funds. Unfortunately, too many businesses do not follow this biblical principle and this is a big mistake. Treat borrowed funds the same as your own, and you will end up with a much more successful business.

2. Limit your inventory risk.

If you have inventories, look for ways to limit the risk of having perishable inventory or inventory you are stuck with. Look for consignment, where you do not have the inventory risk. Drop shipment direct from the manufacturer is a great way to limit inventory risk. Think out of the box to find other ways to keep your product available without laying out a fortune in advance or having to worry about storage and liability for product that may not keep its value.

Although most people thought we had to take a lot of inventory risk at hotels.com, we actually had very low inventory risk. Almost all of our hotel contracts provided for an allocation of rooms with no risk to us. The hotels would commit to allocate a certain number of rooms per night for exclusive sale by us, but if we did not sell them within a certain number of days or hours before check-in they would revert back to the hotel. This is called an allocation or allotment. With this system, we had tons of inventory but no risk.

For the hotels to agree to work with us under this method, they had to see production, or next season they wouldn't continue to provide us this allocation. It also wasn't fair to the hotel to take allocations that we didn't need. So we were very careful to ask only for allocations we needed and made sure we worked hard to sell a very high percentage of each hotel allocation. Then the hotels would be very willing to extend our allocation for another year or expand it based on our projections for growth. This was a very creative way of limiting inventory risk.

Occasionally we would commit to the rooms in advance if we were fairly certain we would sell the rooms and the margin was high enough to justify the added risk. This would be for special events such as the Super Bowl or Mardi Gras. We also sometimes would commit to all of the rooms in a hotel or an entire floor of a hotel in a major city where our demand was many times the number of rooms we contracted for. This was a small percentage of our business, but we did this carefully, were compensated with additional margin, and left plenty of room for error. In short, we limited our inventory risk.

3. Limit your downside.

Before you go into your business or do a transaction, make sure you understand the worst downside you can have. Don't pursue deals where there is a possibility of taking a big loss even if this risk is very small. At the same time, don't ever limit your potential profit: look for deals that have unlimited upside. Always consider the worst-case scenario, regardless of how unlikely it is to occur. In a worst-case scenario, what would happen to your business? How much would you lose? Is there a slight chance that you could be liable for millions of dollars or much more than your profit due to the way you operate your business? Think about how you can limit that risk. I think about risk all the time, as too much risk is what leads many companies to failure. We have always stayed away from any deal that had what is called catastrophic risk – this is risk that will bring the house down because it is so large. You can't take that risk, no matter how slim the chances are that it will really happen. Yet companies take such risks all the time. This is not prudent – there is no reason to ever take catastrophic risk, unless you are covered by insurance for this.

At getaroom.com, one of the ways we limit our downside is by taking on no inventory risk. If the hotel rooms do not sell, they revert back to the hotels within a certain number of hours or days before check-in. We thus have no inventory risk. I have seen many other companies take on a lot of inventory risk and end up stuck with the inventory. As the middleman instead of the hotel, our risk is minimized. Thus, during tough economic periods, we survived and did well, but unfortunately many travel vendors that owned the inventory and could not sell it went into bankruptcy.

Making investments in areas that are not core to your business is often a mistake. Not only is it a distraction from your main focus, but also it can take you out on a limb because you usually don't understand that secondary business well enough to assess and minimize the risk level. By acting just as the middleman between the hotel owner and the customer, we don't take on any risk of a downturn in the economy or other issues that could impact the bottom-line profit of the hotel. We earn our commission regardless of economic conditions or specific issues at a hotel. We thus have limited downside risk but almost unlimited upside potential as our industry is so large. Limit your risk and investment, and your likelihood of success will go way up.

4. Buy insurance.

Make sure you insure your company against liability and other significant business risk. Premiums are small compared to the potential losses. Self-insuring in certain situations can be a valid money-saving technique, however. Self-insuring means you do not take out an insurance policy, saving money on premiums, but you take on the responsibility of paying out claims yourself. If you decide to self-insure, only do so when you know what the worst downside could be, and never do this for liability, no matter how small the risk. When you have analyzed the risk properly, you can use this method effectively, keeping costs low while guarding against catastrophic risk. We self-insure for health insurance, offering our employees health insurance on which we ourselves pay out the claims. We have this administered by a major health insurance provider and we still buy insurance for high potential claims, however low the likelihood of the claim. We thus figured out a way to provide health insurance at a lower cost and at the same time insure against large claims. Never leave yourself vulnerable to catastrophic claims for which you are uninsured.

5. Watch cash flow.

Set up your business to have good cash flow so you are not always scrambling to make payroll and pay your bills. At hotels.com, we went from a startup business with terrible cash flow and on the verge of going out of business to a business with great cash flow by changing our business model. At first, we worked on a commissionable model: we made the bookings, but no money changed hands until the customer arrived at the hotel. The customer paid the hotel, and then we had to wait to receive our commission.

Since many hotels were not prompt in paying (and many didn't pay at all!), we changed our model to a merchant model. In this model, we contracted with the hotel for a net rate for the hotel rooms and sold the rooms at a marked-up higher rate. We no longer had to chase commissions since we received the full payment in advance from our customers. From that payment, we kept our commission and paid the hotel the net rate.

There was more to the new model than being guaranteed that we would be paid our commission. Now our customers were paying us in advance. We went to the hotels and established credit with them and they billed us for the rooms. Our average booking was thirty days in advance. Typically, we were billed by the hotels thirty days after checkout and we had thirty days to pay the invoices. This procedure gave us an automatic ninety-day float. We never had cash flow issues again or needed to borrow funds to run our business. Having good cash flow allows you to focus on running your business instead of focusing your attention on how you are going to pay the next bill.

6. Start small and test.

Most entrepreneurs want to conquer the world in a day. They tell me they want to start a business and make it national or worldwide from day one, including a massive global advertising campaign. They are ready to spend a fortune on marketing their business without having any empirical data proving that their concept works. I tell them that my best piece of advice is to start small, don't invest much initially, and see if your program works in a small test. You can always expand once you know it works from a small test, but if you are incautious and blow through your bank account in a few days or weeks, your business is over. This is usually the best piece of advice I give would-be entrepreneurs.

Test the waters and see if your business model works by trying out your concept in a small geographic area or with limited products. We started with one hotel market and when our business plan was working, we expanded it to six. We worked in just six markets for about two years. We refined our business model and made a great business from these six markets. If we had tried to go out to hundreds of markets initially, we probably would have failed. We would not have had enough product and good deals in each market and our customers would not have seen the value. We would have lost most of our customers.

By focusing on a small number of markets, we were able to go deep into each market and negotiate lots of great values. We had amazing deals in New York, and our customers knew that if they were going to New York or one of our other five markets, they would find great bargains with us. When we widened our offerings to include other cities, we had the resources to expand deeply into more markets because we already had a very solid base in our original six markets. We added the additional markets slowly and methodically, figuring out where the demand was for our customers. We made sure we expanded each market well, with great values in each area of the new destination cities and in each price category.

Don't run the risk of being out of business before you even really get started. When you start small and test your market, you can slowly and methodically figure out your business model – without spending a lot of funds. You may have a great business plan on paper, but it is very different in the real world. I have never been in a business that goes exactly according to the business plan. It is always a circuitous route and ends up very differently from what you originally anticipated. It almost always costs more, takes longer, and is much more difficult than you anticipated. Start small and test your business model and avoid the risk of a quick downfall.

7. Invest conservatively and diversify.

As your business accumulates excess funds, you have funds set aside for payables, or you have taken profits out of your business and are ready to invest those funds, think about the biblical principles of asset allocation and limiting risk. I have seen businesses, charities, and individuals take huge losses because they invested all or most of their eggs in one basket – most recently the fraudulent Bernie Madoff basket. I have seen other businesses play the roulette wheel by taking excess profits and putting all the funds in a high-flying stock and losing it all. I have seen many companies take their funds and invest in high-yield bonds that later defaulted, with the result that the businesses could not make their payables.

High yield usually means high risk. Invest prudently. Company short-term funds should never be invested in anything but very short-term instruments that have the highest ratings, such as government-backed instruments. It is never a wise choice to invest all your net worth in one fund or one stock. Diversify your investments, limit the risk you take with funds held, and focus on the risk at least as much as you focus on the return when investing.

"A prudent man sees danger, and protects himself; but the thoughtless press forward, and are punished" (Proverbs 27:12). When you use the preceding seven tips to follow the biblical principle of limiting risk, you will protect your business from large and unexpected losses.

Seven Ways to Limit Risk

1. Limit your investment. . . . . ☑
2. Limit your inventory risk. . . . . ☐
3. Limit your downside. . . . . ☐
4. Buy insurance. . . . . ☐
5. Watch cash flow. . . . . ☐
6. Start small and test. . . . . ☐
7. Invest conservatively and diversify. . . . . ☐

Be Frugal and Minimize Debt

The rich rule over the poor
and the borrower is servant to the lender.
– Proverbs 22:7

I learned growing up never to waste. My maternal grand-father, David Zang, never left a crumb of food on his plate. At every meal he would take a piece of bread, wipe his plate clean, and eat the bread so as not to waste a drop. He would be very upset if we left food on the plate. He would tell us, "Start with a small serving, and if you are still hungry take more." Living through World Wars I and II and several wars in Israel, he understood the meaning of scarce resources. He abhorred waste and taught that lesson to us vividly. I follow this principal still today. It bothers me to see food left on a plate, and I regularly eat leftovers.

My entire family lived with a strong ethos of conservation of resources and avoidance of waste. My parents always looked at the prices before buying. If an item was not on sale, we would wait for the sale before buying it. I have a hard time paying retail for anything. Why pay full price when it will be going on sale in a few days or weeks? I'd rather just wait, or buy something else that is on sale now. I always look for a coupon code before buying something online. I feel better about the purchase when there is a value.

I have applied this same frugality to my businesses. In every company I founded, I developed a culture of no waste. No fancy lunches, expensive offices, first-class travel, or other waste. My partner Dave grew up the same way and shares my passion for not wasting. When we initially sold hotels.com to USA Networks, which became IACI, Interactive Corp., it was a clash of cultures. They had retreats with the management of the companies they controlled at fancy hotels and were not accustomed to our level of frugality. We refused to pay these prices and either negotiated free rooms or a special rate. While their executives traveled first class or on a company plane, we traveled coach and usually found a way to get the tickets for free. We couldn't understand why any company would take on such expenses. After a while, they finally figured out that we don't spend on anything we don't absolutely need and respected our frugality.

> Develop a culture of no waste. Don't spend on anything you don't absolutely need.

Years ago when I was in the airline business, we had an office in New York on 44th and Lexington for the company we called Travelers Choice. It was an older building close to Grand Central Station that housed a lot of travel companies. We had a good deal on rent and I found a place to buy used furniture that was attractive, functional, and cost a fraction of what we would have paid for new. I was on a JetBlue flight from Miami going back to New York one morning and started talking to the lady sitting next to me. She told me she was with a New York travel agency and I told her I was with Travelers Choice. Her eyes lit up and she was very excited to tell me that not only was she a customer, but she had been in our offices a few months ago to visit one of our agents. She said that she was very loyal to our company and wouldn't look anywhere else for the products we offered.

I asked her what made her such a devoted customer and she told me that when she visited our offices in New York, she was so impressed at how frugal we were. She admired the used furniture, photocopying on both sides of the page, using pencils to the very end, and everyone dedicated and working hard. She told me she knew we would be in business a long time because we watched the bottom line and had dedicated staff. She said she was uncomfortable doing business with high-flying companies that waste and live on the edge. "So many of them go out of business because they don't care about expenses," she said. She told me she knew there was no way that would happen to Travelers Choice, and she was right. We watched the bottom line like hawks and scrutinized every penny of expense. We do the same thing today.

In running a business you need to set a philosophy throughout the organization of watching costs. Most companies fail due to runaway expenses. It is very tough to change employee expectations and habits once they are in a culture of excessive spending. A sensible attitude toward spending must come from the top: you can't have the CEO wasting and expect your employees to be thrifty. But if the CEO is watching every expense, then employees can't expect to spend more than the CEO.

I look for ways to cut costs as much as I look for ways to grow the top line (i.e., gross income). Both result in higher earnings. We constantly look for efficiencies: automation to reduce manual labor, reducing credit card fee costs, reducing fraud losses, cutting phone and Internet charges, and more. The two largest expenses tend to be marketing/advertising and employee costs. We have strategies to keep both of these in line.

We set up compensation to reward sales employees based on production. While we pay a base salary, market managers only earn higher levels if the company does well. We limit annual salary increases to no more than the cost of living. During tough periods, we impose salary caps. Every new hire needs to be justified by the incremental revenue the prospective employee will bring in above the salary he or she will be paid. All of our employees are also equity owners of the company so they understand that if the company is excessive on compensation and other items, the value of the business and hence their own interest is worth less. At the same time, we make sure we are fair to our employees. At hotels.com, most employees earned more in their stock options than they did in salary. We worked as a team together to create value. At getaroom.com, all employees also have stock options and the more that flows to the bottom line, the more those options are worth to the employees.

The other big expense is advertising and marketing. While many companies in the online space spend much of their revenues on marketing, we strive to keep our marketing spend at a small single-digit percentage of revenues. You need to be creative in finding unique ways to market your company without breaking the bank on advertising. So many companies in our space went out of business because they could only grow by increasing ad spend. They never figured out a way to grow without expensive advertising. Key to our success has been setting up programs for growth without spending ad dollars.

To put cost savings in context, it is important to understand that companies are valued on a multiple of their earnings. Based on our growth rate, our company is worth many times our annual earnings amount. Depending on interest rates, multiples in the public markets for comparable businesses, and other factors, this multiple can range from high single digits to as much as twenty to thirty times our earnings. Therefore, for every dollar we spend, our company loses a multiple of that amount in net worth. If we save a million dollars a year from watching the bottom line closely, we've just created a multiple of that million dollars in additional value for the company.

Key to success in your company is being able to grow your top line (gross income, so named because it is generally the top line of a company's balance sheet) while growing the expense line at a much slower rate. This is the most exciting phase of a company's growth. You passed the startup phase and are finally profitable. Now your goal is to grow top-line numbers and keep the incremental expense lower than the top-line growth: this is your visible manifestation of efficiencies and scale at work.

Many companies have failed because they spend too much, go into too much debt and don't have tight control over expenses. Most businesses do not watch their bottom lines carefully and this leads to their demise. Excessive debt and leverage led to the great recession of 2008 and put many companies out of business.

Be careful not to go into excessive debt. When you run your business conservatively, you are forced to focus more on your cash flow and bottom line. This is the right discipline for running a business and will help you achieve success.

Many entrepreneurs have taken on heavy debt and diluted their interest through raising private equity capital so that they could spend more on marketing. Analysts ask me all the time why we don't spend as much on marketing as our competitors do. When I was president of hotels.com, we spent 2 to 6 percent of our revenues on advertising and marketing. At getaroom.com, we spend less than 1 percent of our revenues on marketing and advertising. This keeps us profitable. My response to these analysts is that spending a lot on marketing and advertising is not what makes a long-term successful business. Very few businesses become successful just by buying more advertising. Real success comes from being honest in your business dealings, building a solid reputation, and thereby attracting loyal long-term customers. You can't buy this with advertising.

At getaroom.com, we started out doing a lot of online advertising as we were growing. We suffered losses for our first three years, mainly due to the advertising expense. As soon as we cut advertising expense to less than 1 percent of revenues, we became profitable. Sales did not suffer. In fact, we are growing faster now than when we spent a lot on advertising. When we curtailed this expense, we found other creative ways to grow the business. We expanded our affiliate program and brought on large partners to whom we supplied inventory. We beefed up our PR by having me go on radio and television as a guest, at no charge to us. We improved our customer retention management (CRM) by enhancing and improving our e-mail campaigns. We did not need the advertising to grow.

Much of our business comes from our affiliate partners, and we keep growing this channel of distribution. These are other companies, mostly travel companies, that sell our hotels. They buy the ads to promote their companies and bring in traffic, but we don't have to pay for this traffic. We only pay them a commission based on production. Transactions are always profitable, since we keep sufficient margin, and there is no up-front cost to acquiring the business. We only pay a commission if a customer makes a purchase; thus, we control our marketing expense.

We do a lot of PR and it is free. I'm on the radio weekly on shows such as KGO radio in San Francisco, and I often appear on television shows such as NBC News and Fox News promoting getaroom.com. While other companies buy thirty-second ads on television and have to repeat the ad many times for consumers to remember it, when I'm on TV it is usually about a ten-minute spot and the listeners get to know me and the company. It is so much more valuable than buying advertising, as consumers are much more attuned to the programming than to the advertising. Best of all, it's free!

When you consciously limit your ad budget, you find other low-cost ways to promote your company. I always test new ideas slowly and make sure they work before I spend more dollars on a marketing program. If the ideas show promise after initial trial runs, I work hard to expand them.

Another common area of overspending is corporate travel. How do you make sure employees limit their travel expenses? The best way I have found is by having the employees pay their own expenses and then seek reimbursement. Yes, they will get reimbursed and won't actually have any personal expense, but when they have to lay out their own funds up front, they treat the money as their own and spend much more carefully. People tend to spend their own dollars more wisely. Employees with corporate credit cards often don't care how much they charge to the company. (How many times have you heard someone wave off a large expense saying, "It doesn't matter – the company is picking up the tab"?) This is just another way to promote a company culture of not wasting.

Whenever my executives want to increase their budget and spend money on something, I require that they at the same time provide an analysis of how there is going to be a payback of the expense in a short period of time. If they can't convince me that we are going to get a decent multiple back from the purchase or expense, I don't approve it. They usually will vet requests from the employees they manage and don't present any spending requests without this analysis. Most of the waste gets eliminated this way.

I also require that employees stick to budgets. My policy is that no one can go over budget unless it is approved in advance. Employees must be disciplined about expenses and the best way to do this is to have a budget and not allow any overages. Of course, we are always giving high praise to those executives whose teams come in under budget.

Minimize debt, watch expenses carefully, and you will be much more likely to succeed.

A Dozen Ways to Run a Tight Ship

1. Grow your top line and watch your expense line. . . . . . ☑

2. Create a corporate culture of conservation
   by setting a good example as the CEO. . . . . ☐

3. No fancy lunches, expensive offices,
   first-class travel or other unnecessary luxury. . . . . . . ☐

4. Look for efficiencies: reducing service fee costs,
   reducing fraud losses, cutting phone and
   Internet charges, and more. . . . . ☐

5. Hire new employees only when
   the new hire will bring in incremental revenue
   above the salary he or she will be paid. . . . . ☐

6. Keep employees invested – literally.
   Give employees stock options in the company
   so that your success is theirs. . . . . ☐

7. Keep advertising expenses in the low single digits
   as a percentage of your revenue. . . . . ☐

8. Think out of the box to have affiliates
   shoulder some of your marketing costs. . . . . ☐

9. Find creative ways to get free PR
   such as by appearing as a guest on radio and TV. . . . . ☐

10. Test before you invest. Make sure new marketing
    ideas work before you spend on a whole program. . . . . ☐

11. Have employees pay their own expenses
    and then seek reimbursement
    so they will treat your money like their own. . . . . ☐

12. No going over budget without prior approval. . . . . ☐

Find Solutions

So shall be My word that goes forth
out of My mouth:
it shall not return to Me emptily,
but will accomplish what I please,
and achieve what I sent it for.
– Isaiah 55:11

When I want to get something accomplished, I require that my employees tell me how to make it happen instead of telling me the many reasons why it can't be done. People are usually afraid of change and leaving their comfort zone. They therefore erect barriers instead of seeking to find solutions. When I hear employees doing this, I immediately stop them and tell them I don't want to hear any more reasons why they can't do the project. I tell them to go and figure out how to get it done. I have found that if you believe in something, it will happen regardless of the difficulty. As the US Army Corps of Engineers used to say during World War II, "The difficult we do immediately. The impossible takes a little longer."[1] Successful entrepreneurs constantly innovate and focus their companies on finding solutions instead of focusing on the barriers.

Focus on how to make it happen instead of on the many reasons why it can't be done.

A few years ago we decided to test television commercials at getaroom.com. We had set a limited budget of $10,000 to produce and bring to market three commercials. We interviewed several major advertising agencies and they wanted anywhere from $150,000 to $500,000 to produce our commercials. They gave us elaborate proposals including bringing on a writer, director, producer, permit expeditor, and more. Just reading through their proposals was exhausting. I was amazed at how complex they made a process that I viewed as simple. I had already produced several sets of television commercials while at hotels.com, so I knew how the process worked. All that was required, it seemed to me, was to systematically go through several steps.

Instead of hiring these expensive firms, I found another way: I wrote, directed, produced, and acted in our commercials. I found a video production company willing to work within our budget. I called a hotel and asked permission to film in their lobby. No permits, producers, actors, directors, and other expensive talent. It was all free. We filmed in the lobby of the hotel and in the elevator. It took a couple of hours of filming several takes and a few weeks of editing. We already had our background theme music, which is in the public domain. We used inexpensive film and produced the three commercials, including the editing,

---

1.   Bruce Bohle, ed., *The Home Book of American Quotations* (New York: Gramercy, 1967), p. 35.

copying, and sending out the final version, for less than our $10,000 budget. Almost everyone told me why this could not be done within our budget, but I didn't believe them.

I had a similar experience when we worked on our first set of television commercials at hotels.com. Although we paid more than $10,000 to produce them, we still paid a fraction of what most companies were paying to produce commercials. Instead of paying for expensive actors, my partner and I acted in the commercials. This cost less and it was great PR that the founders of the company were acting in their own commercials. We filmed our first commercial in the Orange Bowl in Miami. We needed to make the stadium look full and fill up a section of the stadium. Instead of spending a lot of money recruiting people, we sent a couple of employees to the beach in South Beach and handed out flyers that offered the opportunity to appear in a nationally televised TV commercial. The flyer stated to just show up at the Orange Bowl at 7 AM on the given day, sign a waiver, and sit in the stands. On the day of filming there was a line down the block early in the morning at the Orange Bowl of all the people who wanted to be in the commercial. We thus filled the stadium for free.

One of the most expensive parts of the process of filming a commercial is purchasing the film itself. Instead of using the latest and highest resolution film, we used an inexpensive film that had a tint. While most companies viewed this as an inferior product, we viewed it as a way to save money and we believed it would not have that much impact. As it turned out, not only did the inexpensive film not have a negative impact, but it made the commercials stand out in the marketplace. Everyone else had the slick, high-resolution film and so looked the same. We had an older-looking, less sharp commercial – but it stood out. It looked different from all the others. People remembered it, and it cost a fraction of what the competition was paying. This was just another example of finding solutions to problems and finding creative ways to work within limited budgets.

The entrepreneur often has a big advantage over the big company: being nimble and fast. Streamline decision making so you can react quickly to changing market conditions. Fight bureaucracy whenever it rears its ugly head. Bureaucracies kill companies. Meetings, chains of command, layers of approval – these all stifle productivity. You need to figure out a way to respond quickly.

The biblical story of King Solomon is a classic example of creative problem solving. People came to him from all over the world to solve problems they could not figure out on their own. He was blessed with great wisdom, and when confronted with issues, he thought outside the box. The most famous story of his penetrating wisdom was when two women came to him with a baby, each claiming the baby was hers. Knowing that the true mother would not let her baby be hurt, his judgment was to slice the baby in half and give each claimant half of the baby. One of the women cried out, "Do not harm the child! I renounce my claim on him!" King Solomon knew that the true mother was the one who did not want the baby to be hurt. This was a creative way of finding a solution to a problem. Think about this when confronted with difficult issues – think outside the box and creatively. Think how to find a solution, not what the difficulties are.

How to Find
Out-of-the-Box Solutions

When you set a limited budget,
you will be forced to find creative solutions to get things done
within it. Here are some steps to take and questions to
ask yourself as you look for ways to accomplish
what others might tell you is impossible.

☞ Start by clearly identifying the problem that
   needs solving.

☞ Talk about potential solutions with others.
   Find experts.

☞ Write down all the conventional solutions.
   Will any work?

☞ Can you resolve part of the issue?

☞ Try a different approach that no one has used
   before. Have others solved the problem? How?

☞ Are there international solutions?

☞ Don't spend time talking about
   why it can't be done. Spend your time talking
   about ways to get it done.

Be Humble:
Accept and Encourage Criticism

If it concerns the scorners, He scorns them,
but to the humble He extends grace.
– Proverbs 3:34

I learned to be humble and accept criticism from studying Proverbs. "He who loves knowledge loves correction, but he who is arrogant hates criticism" (Proverbs 12:1). The Bible teaches us to be humble. Pride gets in the way of success. We all make mistakes. Never think you are always right. Accept and encourage criticism, especially from your employees, who understand the business better than anyone. My best ideas come from customers and employees. We read every customer and employee suggestion carefully. I see so many managers and CEOs who don't listen to their employee suggestions. This is a big mistake. Creating an environment that allows suggestions and criticism can greatly improve your productivity and allow employees and customers to feel more part of the business. "Where there is no wise direction, a people falls, but with ample advice comes salvation" (Proverbs 11:14).

At hotels.com, we kept a sealed suggestion box into which employees could put comments anytime. We asked employees not to put their names on the suggestions, so management would not know where each comment came from. Many employees felt intimidated and weren't comfortable making suggestions or criticisms publicly or even under their own names for fear of repercussions. We therefore had an anonymous system and constantly received suggestions this way. We read them, took them seriously, and made many changes to the company and site based on these suggestions. No one understands your company better than your employees and customers: encourage them to give feedback. We received thousands of customer comments, both good and bad. We still receive an amazing amount of customer feedback. We receive input by mail, e-mail, fax, through our call center, and through social media. We read every one of these messages and have them summarized for management. Many features of the current versions of our websites came about as a result of these comments.

I'm very fortunate to have had a great business partner for over thirty years. We have been through many businesses together and serve as each other's checks and balances. I scrutinize his work and he scrutinizes mine. I always send him copy to review for his comments and he does the same with me. We constantly give each other criticism and feedback. Dave and I met at the Cornell Law School. We weren't that friendly until one day in our third and final year of law school. Dave was eavesdropping on a conversation I was having over lunch with another classmate about our travel plans after we finished law school. We were discussing traveling around the world, starting with Japan and Thailand. Dave asked if he could join us. We had a lively discussion about the travel plans and the three of us decided to travel around the world together after graduation.

We met Dave in Japan and continued from there to China, Southeast Asia, and many other destinations. We became best friends on the trip and had long discussions about our ambitions, business ideas, ethics, values, and more. I was impressed with Dave's passion to succeed. After the trip, Dave went to Dallas to work with the large law firm of Johnson & Swanson and I went to Los Angeles to work with the large law firm of Gibson, Dunn & Crutcher. We were both itching to find the right business to go into. Law practice brought in a nice paycheck but we knew we were never going to be very wealthy practicing law. We were both entrepreneurs. We wanted to be in the position our clients were in instead of working for them.

Dave bought some rental houses and small apartment units in Dallas. He found a way to buy these with almost no money down. He would then rent them out with the rental income exceeding the mortgage and other costs. We discussed expanding this. The problem was that markets were cyclical, buildings have unforeseeable maintenance issues, and he had to chase tenants for the rent. It also required a lot of capital to do this on a large scale, which we didn't have. I suggested something more portable – cars. I love cars and was surprised to see how much lower the prices were in Dallas for used Mercedes Benz sports cars than they were in Los Angeles. I went to visit Dave in Dallas, found a great deal on a 450 SL convertible, and bought it. When I went back to Los Angeles, I placed an ad in the *Dallas Morning News* to sell the car, which I had left behind with Dave. He took the calls and a few weeks later sold the car for $1,200 profit.

To show me how serious he was about going into business together, he flew to Los Angeles and personally handed me the $600 in cash that was my share of the profit. He said, "This is just the start – let's figure out what makes money and go into business together." I was impressed at his passion. He was never short of ideas. He was relentlessly determined to succeed. He liked working hard and making money. He was just like me. I decided it would be much better to have a partner to brainstorm with and make money with than to go it alone. It is great to have someone with whom to share the success and develop new ideas. We thought alike and he always had constructive and valid criticism. We respected each other's drive, values, and ethics. Choosing Dave as my partner and marrying my wife were the two most important and best decisions I have made in my life.

Dave and I have been partners now for over thirty years. We never have had a conflict and we trust each other's judgment. We both put in equal effort and have similar drive, even after thirty years. We still seek – and respect – each other's advice. We still solicit each other's feedback and appreciate the constructive criticism. It makes us much better. Find the right partner and you will be much more than the sum of the parts.

Our next idea was to buy used sports cars in Dallas and then ship them to Los Angeles, where the prices were much higher. The problem was we could not do this in high volume. Furthermore, if we needed repairs on the cars, it was expensive. Around that time the airlines started getting aggressive in giving out free tickets, and Dallas was the ideal market for acquiring these. American Airlines was based there, and it was a major hub for Delta and other carriers. Dave could acquire the free tickets in Dallas, and I could sell them in Los Angeles, where trips are longer and fares are higher. Now we had no bulky cars to ship, just pieces of paper. No warehouses or parking lots were needed to store the goods. And the tickets bought and sold fast so cash flow was good. Many people travel and there was a huge market. Our next business adventure was in the works. It was a lot of fun talking through each of these ideas until we found the right business. We each poked holes in the other's ideas until we found the business we couldn't poke holes in.

It is a natural tendency to be stubborn and not want to listen to criticism. We tend to be protective of our own suggestions and ideas. Yet we are usually much better off when we get feedback from others and make adjustments accordingly. No one is perfect and we all make mistakes: let other people help you find them. Although I usually thoroughly analyze an issue, I prefer to have someone else competent look at my plans and documents before I make them final. If you don't have a business partner, find someone such as a spouse, friend, or professional who can review your work and provide honest criticism. Allow your employees to disagree with your suggestions. Provide an environment in your company that nourishes feedback, both positive and negative.

> No one is perfect and we all make mistakes: let other people help you find them.

Building a strong executive team is a great way to check your work. Encourage your executives to speak up and give feedback and comments. You should only hire executives whose opinions you trust and respect. If you hire executives who are just going to rubber-stamp everything you do, you are doing yourself a great disservice. Find strong-minded executives who think independently, have great ideas, and are willing to confront you. If you don't value their ideas, you either need new executives or you need to be more open to accepting criticism. Also, don't try to be the expert on everything. A good entrepreneur acknowledges that others can do many tasks better. I don't try to program our site or handle HR. There are many people who can do these tasks and others better than I can. We learn from Proverbs to be humble: don't assume you know everything and are an expert at every task. Do what you do best and let others who can perform tasks better handle those tasks. Be humble as the Bible teaches, and give yourself the best chance of success.

Best Ways to Solicit Constructive Criticism

1. Have an anonymous suggestion box.. . . . . ☑

2. Solicit ideas from employees
at every opportunity. . . . . ☐

3. Create an environment
that encourages suggestions.. . . . . ☐

4. Add suggestion links on your website.. . . . . ☐

5. Have a team that reads and complies
with customer feedback. . . . . ☐

6. Actively read and respond to Facebook
and other social marketing comments. . . . . ☐

7. Take customer surveys. . . . . ☐

8. Run employee contests to encourage
suggestions and creativity. . . . . ☐

9. Ask your customers, partners,
and others for feedback. . . . . ☐

10. Acknowledge those who
come up with great suggestions.. . . . . ☐

10

Have the Highest Level of Customer Service

Love your neighbor as yourself.
– Leviticus 19:18

Customer service issues are paramount in the travel business: flight delays, lost luggage, noisy rooms, housekeeping issues, and more. I set up a very simple standard for customer care: put yourself in your customers' shoes and treat them as you want to be treated. I learned this from Leviticus 19:18: "Love your neighbor as yourself." While many companies struggle with how to handle customer service, following this standard is the best way to build a long-term loyal customer base. The great sage Hillel, when challenged to state the entire Bible while standing on one foot, stated, "What is hateful to you, do not do to your fellow; this is the whole Law. The rest is but commentary" (Babylonian Talmud, *Shabbat* 31a).

I learned from Rabbi Hillel and the Bible how to build a business with great customer service.

The key is to provide the level of service and the handling of customer service issues that I would expect if I were the customer. This is how we train employees to handle customer issues. We all prefer to patronize businesses that are fair on returns and exchanges and that treat us well. We refer our friends there. When we launched getaroom.com, top customer service was a great competitive advantage in a marketplace where most competitors outsource their call centers overseas to save costs and where it is difficult to find a high level of customer service. We are constantly told by our partners that we have the highest level of customer service in the industry. We do not outsource our customer service overseas but handle it all within the US. The high level of customer service has differentiated us in the marketplace and enabled us to build a loyal customer base. Customers patronize businesses that treat them well and make them comfortable. Most companies compete just on price, but price is only one factor among many that a consumer takes into account in choosing where to buy. Gaining your customers' trust is a huge asset to your business and helps you retain your customers and find new ones.

We hear every day from customers that they dealt with other companies that had poor customer service and that they will never do business with them again. For every customer who is pleased with your customer service, you will receive not only continued repeat business from that customer but also referrals. Our average customer books a couple of times a year,

> Use a very simple standard for customer care: put yourself in your customers' shoes and treat them as you want to be treated.

so one satisfied customer can easily lead to ten more bookings over the next several years, and there is no acquisition cost for that customer.

I learned long ago that there is never a bad customer service situation. Things happen in the travel industry and there will always be issues. No matter how hard you work at customer service, there are always going to be upset customers. We don't view this as a *problem*, but rather as an opportunity to turn the situation around and build loyal customers. Anyone upset about a service issue who later becomes pleased at how we handled the situation will usually become a customer for life. Such customers have the comfort level that when there is a problem, we will get it resolved to their satisfaction.

So many companies, especially in the travel business, where so much can go wrong, have terrible service. I have seen people at airline counters who waited in line for close to an hour and a half only to be told they missed the cutoff for the flight. When they argued that they were there ninety minutes prior, but were stuck in the airline's long line, the agent just responded that they missed the flight and it's not the airline's fault that there was a long line. When they asked for a refund, the agent told them that the ticket is nonrefundable. When they asked to be moved to another airline, the agent told them that the airline does not have an agreement with the other airlines. Of course any such customer would never fly that airline again and will tell everyone he or she knows about the horrible experience. I see situations like this all the time. Treating customers well has enabled us to succeed in a very competitive marketplace.

By focusing on the above standard of treating your customers as you want to be treated and putting yourself in their shoes, you can beat the competition and gain loyal clients. Remember how much it cost you to bring in a customer in the first place. Why lose one from poor customer service?

Top Ways to Turn an Angry Customer into a Loyal Customer for Life

1. Listen. Customers often just want someone to pay attention to them.

2. Be empathetic and apologize for the issue. Make your customers feel important, because they are.

3. Offer a rebate.

4. Offer a discount off the next reservation/purchase/service.

5. Upgrade the customer.

6. Offer a certificate of value, such as free movie tickets or a dining credit.

7. Thank the customer for his or her patience and understanding.

8. Give the customer extra loyalty points.

9. Ask the customer whether he or she is happy with the resolution.

10. Give the customer a direct contact at the company to be in touch with if there is ever an issue.

Part 3

Building and Maintaining
a Solid Business Reputation

11

Be Transparent with Customers

You shall have just balances, just weights.
– Leviticus 19:36

Business owners are constantly confronted with dilemmas: How much do you disclose to your customers? Do you deliver exactly what was ordered or substitute something inferior to make a higher profit? Do you put in slightly less weight than the amount your customers believe they are paying for? Do you charge more than you agreed to charge? Do you refund less? The answers to these questions are easy when you follow the Bible's guidance.

Even if your customers won't find out, don't cheat them. "Do not...put a stumbling block before the blind" (Leviticus 19:14). This means not to take advantage when the other party doesn't know or see what you are doing. We are often confronted with situations where we could increase profits by cutting corners or otherwise taking advantage of customers in ways that they won't know about. Why not increase profits by using a cheaper material or a second-hand product? Why not use lower-cost components even though the customer believes you are using high-end components? Don't put a stumbling block before the blind: don't cheat your customers, even if they don't know about it. It does not matter whether or not they are with you and watching you. It's wrong, plain and simple.

I recently needed ink cartridges for my printer and searched online for the best deal. I was excited to find one company that had what I needed for much less than any other company I could find. I promptly ordered four cartridges because they were such a good deal. When the cartridges arrived, I installed one in my printer, but the ink came out lumpy. I took that one out but the same thing happened with the second one. I called the company up and after being on hold for over thirty minutes, I finally spoke with a representative who rudely told me, "Too bad, you bought refurnished cartridges and they are nonrefundable." I asked where it said they were refurbished and the agent responded that the information was on the website. I went back to look at the site, and in tiny print, hidden from plain view, it indeed said that the cartridges were refurbished. Nowhere in the checkout process was this disclosed. I didn't see this when I made my purchase and neither would most consumers. This company knows people will not see the word *refurbished*, yet they sell these products by misleading the consumer and failing to reasonably disclose important information about their product, simply to make a profit. This is just one example of putting a stumbling block before the blind.

Extra fees are a major issue in the travel industry, where there are resort fees, cleaning fees, baggage fees, carry-on baggage fees, and more. Although the airline industry is heavily regulated, and there have been several sets of regulations regarding fee disclosures, the lodging industry is not as heavily regulated. Consumers often complain that they were not aware of extra or hidden fees. We have a practice of making such fees clear: we clearly and in bold show the resort fee before customers enter the confirmation page and again before they confirm the transaction. We then highlight this yet another time on the confirmation notice. To follow the principal of not putting a stumbling block before the blind, not only do we disclose this information on our site, but we take steps to make sure the customer clearly sees it. We could have hidden it in descriptions and not shown the charge until after the reservation is confirmed, but instead we take active steps to make sure the customer sees it (as opposed to taking active steps to make sure the customer does not see it, which is all too common).

Every industry has its own examples of such transparency issues, and I can't cover them all specifically here, but I don't need to: when you follow the Bible these issues become easy. You naturally make sure nothing is hidden from your customers but rather make clear and full disclosures. Many companies struggle with determining the level of disclosure, but when you answer to a higher authority, you just take steps to make sure there is nothing hidden. You make sure customers always know exactly what they are paying for and how much it will cost, before they commit to the transaction.

There is a discussion in the Mishnah about the prohibition of deceiving the buyer about the contents of a product or package, and what constitutes deception: "A seller may not mix the product of one field into an order for

> When you answer to a higher authority, you simply make sure customers always know exactly what they are paying for and how much it will cost, *before* they commit to the transaction.

the product of another field" (Mishnah, *Bava Metzia* 4:11). The Talmud in its commentary on the Mishnah continues to discuss various deceptive practices that are forbidden because they make merchandise appear more valuable than it really is. There are examples of making animals appear to be in much better condition than they really are or painting utensils to improve their appearance (Babylonian Talmud, Bava Metzia 60a–b). We learned from this Talmud to be honest with our customers and not hide the true nature of what we are selling.

The Talmud still speaks clearly to us today. Although most of us don't deal in livestock nor paint wooden vessels to hide their flaws, we can certainly relate to modern practices that put a stumbling block before the blind or deceive the buyer as to what is really being sold. Hiding defaults in a home that you are selling, selling a bogus investment product just to make a commission, putting false labels on products, using inferior products, selling second-hand merchandise as new, and putting the best fruit on top to hide the rotten fruit below are just a few examples.

Stay transparent, be clear about what you are selling, talk straight with your customers, and never put a stumbling block before the blind. Not only is it the right thing to do, but customers will reward you for it with their loyalty.

Best Practices for Transparency

- Offer a full and complete product description. . . . . ☑
- Never mislead customers about the origin or components of the product. . . . . ☐
- Never substitute a different product for what was ordered. . . . . . ☐

- Don't hide product flaws. . ☐
- Make sure any extra fees, taxes, or shipping charges are clear up front. . . . . . ☐
- Make any extra fees bold and prominent. . . . . ☐
- Give customers exactly what they are ordering. . . ☐

Take the High Road

When you make an agreement with
your neighbor to buy or sell property,
don't take advantage of each other.
– Leviticus 25:14

I n business, there is always the temptation to cheat. This
is true not only in running your business, but in doing
any kind of transaction between two parties. We all have
the evil inclination and the temptation to do anything
to earn a higher profit. We are given the opportunity – and the
responsibility – to choose which path to go down: following our
evil inclination and taking advantage of the other side or taking
the high road and being honest. In a business setting, when we
are tempted by profit, these choices can truly test us. Can we
overcome temptation and remain honest even if it means lower
profits (at least in the short run), or do we take advantage of our
neighbor for a higher profit?

Think about it: this is the true measure of a person. It is only
when we are in such a tempting setting, faced with this great

desire to go for the higher profit by not being honest, that our character can be judged. This is why it is so important to make the right choice and be honest when you are in this position – this is a real measure of character.

We learn from the *Mechilta*, a midrashic commentary of ethics and spirituality on the book of Exodus, that "If one is honest in his business dealings and people esteem him, it is accounted to him as though he had fulfilled the whole Bible" (*Mechilta*, Beshalach 1). This is how important being honest in business is, and this should be the backbone of your business outlook. I'm constantly confronted with tough questions about deals. I could easily look away and take the deal even though I know it isn't completely honest. But when I think of this Midrash, the answer to the dilemma is clear.

This all stems from the words in Leviticus 19:18: "Love your neighbor as yourself." If you love your neighbor as you love yourself, you won't cheat him. A business setting is your test to see if you can follow this basic tenet of the Bible when tempted to do the opposite. When you refer often to these and other words from Leviticus 19, tough dilemmas become easy. Companies that didn't pass basic ethical tests and instead succumbed to operating unethically are no longer in existence. Who would be comfortable doing business with them? Remember WorldCom and Enron? People want to do business with other honest people and honest businesses.

In the Babylonian Talmud, *Shabbat* 31a, there is a rabbinical discussion of the questions one is asked at the end of one's days in the heavenly court. These ultimate questions show us what is most important in life and give us a yardstick for measuring true success in life. The first question we will be asked is whether or not we were honest in business. The Bible places an emphasis on character and teaches that the most important thing a person can do in life is to be honest, especially when the temptation is to do the opposite. At the end of the day, it is not the fact of achieving wealth that defines success (although Webster's dictionary gives that definition), but how that wealth was obtained. If it was obtained dishonestly, it is meaningless. "Better is the poor person who walks in his integrity than he who is crooked and rich" (Proverbs 28:6). The Bible measures success by asking whether we keep our promises, have personal integrity, and put honesty above profit. When tempted with profitable but ethically questionable deals, walk away. Fundamental to succeeding in business is being honest.

> When tempted with profitable but ethically questionable deals, walk away. Fundamental to succeeding in business is being honest.

We recently changed our accounting system and did not realize that it impacted two of our partners. We accidentally paid them twice for a month of transactions. We might not have found this out until our year-end audit, at which point it might have been too late to go back to these partners and make the correction. One of the affected partners called me and asked if I was aware of the double payment. I thanked him for pointing this out, investigated what happened, and discovered that he was right. Our comptroller, account manager, and everyone else who dealt with this partner was not aware of this double payment. We did a thorough audit and found one other partner to whom the same thing had happened. When I confronted the other partner with the news that we had paid twice, I could tell from the response that this partner already knew about it but had hoped we would not discover the double payment. Imagine how I feel about these two partners. One I will always trust; we have started new programs with them that have almost tripled their business. The other one I know I can't trust completely and I have been hesitant to expand business with him. I hold the honest partner in high esteem and have such great respect for his character. He will have a great hearing in the final court of justice.

There is a simple rule to follow if you want to stay on the straight and narrow: always act as if you are being watched. Your customer overpays you. You receive a refund twice. You are at the cash register and are given a $100 bill instead of a $10 bill. Do you keep the money that was mistakenly given you, or do you give it back? Who will know? When you realize that Someone above is always watching you, the answer is easy. You act differently and work under a higher standard. You run your business and personal life honestly all the time.

I am constantly confronted with situations where a customer or partner makes an honest mistake. A customer overpays. You know the double payment to you will increase your profits and may not get caught. Your customer made an honest mistake.

You receive a check that is meant for someone else. You could deposit it into your account and keep the funds. It may never be noticed, but you know it does not belong to you.

When you are at the cash register and the cashier gives you the $100 bill instead of the $10 bill, you know that the cashier will likely get fired or be charged the difference after the nightly audit. No one will know that it was not the cashier who took the $90 but the customer. Imagine the injustice to the cashier, who is probably just barely scraping by. In all these situations take the high road. As the Bible tells us, "You shall not see your brother's ox or his sheep gone astray and hide yourself from them; you shall surely bring them back to your brother…and so shall you do with his garment; and so shall you do with every lost thing of your brother's, which he has lost and you have found; you may not hide yourself" (Deuteronomy 22:1, 3).

A friend called recently all excited that something great happened to him. He filed his tax return, had a refund of $1000 due from the IRS, and received a check for $10,000 instead. He was convinced that his prayers were being answered. I told him that I hate to be the bearer of bad news, but this is not the way your prayers get answered. I told him that the IRS makes clerical mistakes and that he had an obligation to contact the IRS, find out the source of the error, and return the funds that were not due to him. He told me I was crazy and that I should be happy with his windfall. I strongly suggested he contact his accountant or attorney before he did anything with the check. Unfortunately, he cashed the check and spent the funds on a fancy vacation. He was not too happy when he received the letter a few months later from the IRS pointing out the error and requiring him to return the overpayment. His attorney confirmed that he was obligated to return the money. Now he's depressed and struggling to make the payment.

If he had been honest to begin with, he would never have gotten himself into this situation. He was so convinced this was a present from heaven. I told him that if the doors of his showroom were busting down with customers, this might be an answer to his prayers and a present from heaven. What he received instead was a *test from heaven*. Could he resist the temptation to keep something that was not his, given to him by honest mistake? Could he overcome the great temptation to keep the funds? Unfortunately, he failed the test and is now suffering the consequences.

My friend might have fared better with his test had he kept in mind that Someone is always watching. Ethics of the Fathers 2:1 states: "Know what is above you: An Eye that sees, an Ear that hears, and all your deeds are recorded in a book." Everything we do is being recorded and we are always being watched. When we are mindful of this, we go down the high road. But how do we remind ourselves that we are always accountable for our actions? Many of us have religious or spiritual symbols that remind us that we are never alone. You can find your own symbol to put on your desk, such as a Bible or a calendar with biblical verses, to remind you to follow the ways of the Bible. When you are tempted to do something wrong, look at your symbol and think about the quote above from Ethics of the Fathers. It should remind you that you are never alone and that you have standards you want to live up to.

Those who follow the precepts of the Bible don't embezzle or cheat. Maybe the person being cheated won't find out about it for a long time, but every act of embezzlement is being recorded. Eventually any act of theft will probably be made public and the other person will know. But our Creator knows right away; you also know and have to live with your actions.

I was once in a lengthy contract negotiation with a sizable partner. We went through several versions of the contract with redlines (marked-up changes) and agreed orally to the final provisions. I sent the final redline and clean version of the agreement based upon what we agreed to. When a redline is sent with a clean version, it is understood that any changes you made to the last version are in the redline. The partner sent back an e-mail that everything in this last version of the redlined agreement was acceptable and that he would sign the clean version. He sent the signed agreement and in his cover note wrote that he was attaching the executed agreement based on the terms we agreed to. Most people would not read the agreement again, since they would assume it was the same as the clean version of the last redlined document, with the changes accepted. I quickly scanned the agreement and nothing looked different. I just had a hunch that I should look at the agreement more closely and read every page and word carefully.

To my shock, I found that my negotiating partners had changed several words in the document that significantly changed the terms of the contract. They changed the word "will" to "may," which no longer obligated them to the terms. They changed "will be required" to "will not be required." They changed "after" to "before." These were material changes. We had specifically agreed to the language in the final redlined document. This partner wrote in his e-mail that the changes in the last redlined document were acceptable. His cover note with the signed agreement stated that the agreement was based on the terms we agreed to. They never discussed making these additional changes with me and never gave me any indication that they made the change. They purposely tried to deceive me and change the terms that we agreed to. They tried to hide the changes by not sending a redlined version and by writing that the terms of the last redlined document were acceptable.

I was furious. I read the contract word for word several times to make sure nothing else was changed. I then called the partner to ask why he changed the terms we agreed to and didn't give me another redline version or make any indication of the change. His response was that they couldn't accept the terms and so he changed it. He said although we had an oral deal, it was not signed yet. He should have stuck to his oral agreement, but nonetheless, if he was making a change, he had a moral obligation to tell me about it. To try to trick me by sneaking in the change is what the Bible frowns upon. If I had not had this hunch and gone through the agreement, I wouldn't have known about the change until perhaps a year later, when I would have noticed their not following what I thought the deal was. Then I would have read the contract and I would have (rightly!) felt taken advantage of and deceived.

The moral of this story is first – read the actual document before you sign it, regardless of having read another copy of what you believe is the same document. Before you sign the document, read every page and word carefully. The only binding contract is the one you signed, and you are obligated to read every word before you sign the original. Be sure to read the original, not a copy of it. I also recommend that both parties initial every page, as I have seen others fraudulently try to substitute pages.

I told this partner that this is not the way I do business and that we would only accept the deal under the terms that we had agreed to. I was ready to walk away from a big deal. I was dealing with the CEO of a large company and never would have thought that someone in this position would be so unscrupulous. When he responded that they would only go through with the deal based on the signed version they sent us, I walked away. Even though the terms they signed still would have been an acceptable deal for us, although not nearly as favorable, I didn't want to tolerate such unethical behavior. After two months they came back to the table and signed the original terms we had agreed to.

Even if this CEO had deceived me into signing this document, he never really would have gotten away with this. His actions were being watched even though I could not see this; his actions were being watched and recorded. He will have to answer on the final Day of Judgment to his actions and way of doing business. The company never reached its potential. I'm sure many others didn't do business with them because of their way of doing business. Don't be like this CEO – be honest and act honestly even if someone is not physically watching you. Act as if there is always someone next to you watching over your shoulder.

Time and again we see that honesty is the best policy, and the reward is not saved only for the world to come. When you take the long view and pass up an apparent opportunity to take advantage of someone in the short-term for material gain, you will ultimately find that honesty actually improves the bottom line and long-term success.

I wrote above about a partner who contacted me to tell me we had paid them twice, after we made an honest mistake due to conversion to a new accounting system. Our partner took the high road and pointed this out to us. They might have gotten away with keeping the overpayment, because it would have taken a while for this to surface in our annual audit. It might have then been too late to do anything about it. Yet our partner took the high road. Our partner passed the heavenly test. We have such high regard for this partner. We enjoy doing business with them and keep expanding our business together. This is what happens when you do business honestly. Your business grows, and you end up with a lot more than you would have if you had come by a short-term gain dishonestly. Take the high road and watch your business grow.

Eight Ethical Principles for a Biblical Business Model

1. Be honest with your customers.. . . . . . . ☑
2. Keep your promises and commitments.. . . ☐
3. Follow the law.. . . . . ☐
4. Maintain integrity through words and action.. . . . . ☐
5. Be accountable. . . . . ☐
6. Be loyal.. . . . . ☐
7. Respect others.. . . . . ☐
8. Be thorough in documents – don't leave anything vague. . . . . ☐

Build a Reputation for Integrity

Better is the poor person who walks in his integrity than he who is crooked and rich.

– Proverbs 28:6

I n building your business there is nothing more important than integrity. When people know you are honest and above board, they want to do business with you because they trust you and are comfortable with you. Once you breach that trust, you cannot get it back. All the advertising in the world won't get you repeat and referral business if you don't have integrity. In the Babylonian Talmud, *Shabbat* 31a, which I referenced earlier and will elaborate on in more detail in the afterword, entitled "The Talmudic Formula for Success and Balance in Life," there is the famous story of the heavenly court and the questions one is asked at the end of one's life. The reason the first question asked in the heavenly court is whether you were honest in your business dealings is that this is the true measure of success in life.

There is no greater temptation to cheat than in a business setting where one can earn more profits. If you can overcome this great temptation, you will reach a high level of character that others esteem. Your customers, employees, and business partners will want to patronize your firm. They enjoy doing business with you because they can trust you. When you are honest, your business grows. You also have the right answer for the heavenly court. We learn in Proverbs that there is nothing greater than your reputation: "A good name is rather to be chosen than great riches, and esteem rather than silver or gold" (Proverbs 22:1). Ecclesiastes 7:1 states that "A good name is better than precious oil."

> All the advertising in the world won't get you repeat and referral business if you don't have integrity.

In my first airline ticket business, most of our business was from referrals. Every person who bought a ticket would refer four or five friends on average. We gave people great values, treated them well, and built a reputation for integrity and great value. Our business flourished. We had sufficient demand from our regular customers and referrals that we barely needed to advertise. The travel agent industry loved us and was very loyal because we always paid our commission and we always paid on time. Many travel vendors were not the greatest at paying commissions, and travel agents would have to chase them to get paid. Since we had a reputation for always paying and always on time, travel agents wanted to work with us. This was in large part, in all of our businesses, how we grew and did well. By being honest and building your reputation for integrity, you can grow your business in the most cost-effective way. This is much better than advertising and spending a fortune on marketing. Let your customers be your marketing arm. Treat them fairly and honestly and they will want to help you.

The airline business was a cutthroat industry. There were few barriers to entry and we found ourselves constantly facing new competitors. The newcomers kept undercutting profits. We knew that if we kept matching the lower pricing, this would end up in a downward spiral that eventually would end up with no profits and going out of business. We made the decision to stop matching every minimal price drop regardless of the competition. Our salespeople kept coming to us complaining that customers were seeing lower pricing elsewhere. We were convinced that price was not the only factor in deciding to do business. Yes, everyone wants a lower price, but they also want good customer service and want to be comfortable that they are going to actually receive the product they paid for.

We told our salespeople that when they heard concerns about being able to get a better price elsewhere, they should just ask customers whether they felt comfortable doing business with the cost-cutting company. "How is their customer service?" we instructed them to ask. "Will you receive what you order?" We explained that our pricing was based on a fixed margin that enabled us to provide the proper level of service, and we guaranteed our product. We instructed our agents to tell customers that we didn't understand how these new companies would be able to stay in business with this pricing and to ask the customers whether they felt it was worth taking such a risk for a few dollars.

Our salespeople argued that we were going to lose our customers, but I reassured them that what mattered most was having a fair price and a reputation for being honest, fair, and providing a great level of service. We had a reputation for delivering our product in a timely and reliable fashion and for providing great customer support. As it turned out, we lost very little business due to others undercutting us. Our pricing still represented good value; it was fair even though sometimes there may have been a competitor that undercut us by a few dollars, and our customers still patronized us. We stayed in business while many of those trying to compete with us based on price alone failed. We maintained our profit level, kept providing great customer support, and the competition was a minimal deterrent to our success.

The key was in our trustworthiness. Keep in mind that low pricing is not the only value proposition you can offer. When you are known for your integrity, honesty, reliability, excellent customer service, and stability, you have the tremendous asset of credibility in the market. This separates you from the pack and gives consumers a solid reason to choose your firm over others. Build a great reputation by following these biblical principles and you will be on your way to success because people will want to do business with you.

Top Ways to Build Your Integrity

1. Be fair in advertising. . . . . ☑

2. Always be honest with customers. . . . . ☐

3. Follow through on anything you promise. . . . . ☐

4. Treat customers well –
   the customer is almost always right. . . . . ☐

5. Be polite and courteous. . . . . ☐

6. Avoid conflicts of interest. . . . . ☐

7. Keep your standards and practices consistent. . . ☐

8. Keep confidential matters confidential. . . . . . . ☐

9. Maintain an employee handbook
   and have employees sign that they read it. . . . . ☐

10. Lead by example and train your employees
    to follow these principles. . . . . ☐

14

Obey the Law

Pray for the peace of the government,
since but for the fear of it,
men would swallow each other alive.
– Ethics of the Fathers 3:2

We learn from the Mishnah, in the book Ethics of the Fathers, that we are obligated to follow the laws of the government. The Mishnah is teaching us that biblical law requires us to obey secular law. Thus those who violate the civil or criminal laws enacted by their government are violating the laws of the Bible.

This means that being a law-abiding citizen is more than just one's civic duty; it is one's religious obligation as well. Taxes, civil law, even the rules of the road are our responsibility to uphold.

Some people follow the rituals of their religion scrupulously, but are lax when it comes to following civil laws. This is not acceptable behavior according to the Bible. Make sure you follow the laws and regulations of your industry. Engage professionals when necessary to make sure you are in compliance. It is never worth the risk of breaking the law and jeopardizing your business.

Not only does the Bible teach us to be honest in business, but it also teaches us not to support or encourage those who are violating this principle. In the Talmud, we learn that "One must not buy from the shepherds kids of goats, wool, or milk, and not from fruit watchmen wood and fruits," and that any transaction in which the seller asks that the goods be hidden is forbidden (Babylonian Talmud, *Bava Kama* 10:9).

When we know that workers have stolen goods from their employer, we are obligated not to purchase such goods, as to do so would support this dishonest act. It encourages them to continue this dishonest behavior because they know they have a customer for the goods. The great sage Maimonides informs us that "It is prohibited to buy from a thief any property he has stolen, such buying being a great sin, since it encourages criminals and causes the thief to steal other property. For if the thief finds no buyer he will not steal" (*Mishneh Torah*, Laws of Theft 5:1).

Thieves can only succeed if they have a market to sell their stolen goods. The larger the market, the more they are likely to steal and encourage others to steal as well. You have an obligation to stay away from this, for if you buy stolen goods, you act against the Bible in several ways: first by buying stolen goods, which is forbidden; second by being an accomplice to the thief, since you complete his forbidden act by helping him earn a profit from his theft; and third by encouraging the thief to do it again, because you helped create a market for the stolen product. With one selfish and improper act, you commit at least three sins. "Whoever partners with a thief hates his own soul" (Proverbs 29:24).

> Being a law-abiding citizen is more than just one's civic duty; it is one's religious obligation as well.

This biblical principle extends beyond stolen goods. The same principal applies if the goods were produced or acquired in other ways that were illegal or unethical, such as by exploiting workers. If you know a factory is cheating and exploiting its workers or otherwise harming them, you have an obligation not to purchase goods from this factory. Again, by purchasing goods from this factory, you are creating a market for their goods made by taking advantage of workers. You thereby are accepting their unethical practices and encouraging them to continue this.

The same principle also extends to doing business with entities or countries that are committed to terrorism or other abhorrent conduct. Aside from the possibility of violating sanctions and laws prohibiting such conduct, you also have an ethical obligation not to support companies or countries that act unethically or that are committed to harming innocent people. Unfortunately, when it comes to economic and business settings, too many people are casual about these issues and are willing to overlook others' wrongdoing if they stand to profit from it. The biblical way is not only to act ethically yourself, but to make sure you do not support others acting unethically. You should instead be supporting and doing business with companies that are acting ethically. This shows that you approve of the proper conduct and you thereby encourage them to continue acting in an ethical way.

When you embody ethical integrity and demand it from your associates, your employees and customers will appreciate the principles and ideals you and your company stand for, and they will support and patronize you even more. Just as you patronize honest and ethical companies, so too will others patronize and support you when you are running your business ethically. If you are suspicious of the ethical conduct of a company you are considering doing business with, remember that when it smells or looks like a rat, it probably is.

Ten Safeguards
to Stay on the Right Side of the Law

1. Meet regularly with your attorney
   to update minutes and ensure
   you are in compliance with any
   applicable regulations. . . . . ☑

2. Hire experts when appropriate.. . . . . ☐

3. When hiring professionals,
   find specialists in the area at issue. . . . . ☐

4. Conduct an annual audit of your books. . . . . ☐

5. Conduct a periodic independent audit
   of your business practices. . . . . ☐

6. Ensure employees are following the law.. . . . . ☐

7. Conduct internal audits. . . . . ☐

8. Consult an HR expert and make sure
   you are in compliance with all federal, state,
   and local laws and regulations. . . . . ☐

9. Be careful of the state trap. When you
   do business in more than one state, other
   state laws and taxes may be applicable. . . . . . ☐

10. Be careful internationally.
    Every country has different laws
    and regulations – consult an expert
    in the country you are doing business in. . . . . ☐

Part 4

Keeping a Biblical Perspective on Wealth and Success

15

Prepare for Difficult Economic Times

God gives, and God takes.
– Job 1:21

There will always be difficult economic periods. Recessions, terrorism, serious weather, and other world events are beyond our control. In the fall of 2008, the world economy was falling off a cliff. All of a sudden, major financial institutions started failing. The stock market major indexes lost over 50 percent of their value between the fall of 2007 and the spring of 2009. Housing values plummeted. Lehman Brothers and Bear Stearns ceased to exist. Citibank, Merrill Lynch, and AIG were about to collapse. Money markets were no longer safe. Most of us witnessed our net worth plummet in value and our businesses come to almost a grinding halt.

From a logical perspective, this could never happen. How could the world's largest financial institutions fail? How could major world economies be on the brink of failure? How could so much wealth evaporate in such a short period of time? It all seemed impossible. But from a biblical perspective, it was very possible. "God gives, God takes" (Job 1:21). Just as our Creator has given us wealth, he can take it away. This was the Great Wake-up Call of 2008, not the Great Recession of 2008. Did we wake up? What changes have we made in our lives? What have we learned? How do we handle such difficult periods?

We go to sleep every night and wake up every morning with certain basic assumptions. The sun will rise and set. The moon will go through the lunar cycle. Our houses are on solid foundations and will be in the same place when we wake up. Prior to the fall of 2008, we assumed that when we deposited our hard-earned funds at major brokerage firms or in money market accounts, they were safe. We assumed money markets would never go down in value. We assumed that the checks we wrote from these funds would be honored and paid. We assumed that the cash and securities we held at major investment banks such as Merrill Lynch, Bear Stearns, Lehman Brothers, and others were safe. Who would imagine that the largest and best-known financial institutions in the world would go out of business?

Those of us who invest in and run businesses rely on certain norms to operate. We write checks daily to vendors and have funds in commercial banks to provide cash flow for our businesses. The FDIC insurance limit is not enough to cover our daily cash flows. That's why we bank at Citibank or Merrill Lynch: it was always unthinkable that they could go out of business. How could we possibly operate a business if there was a possibility of those funds being lost? Worldwide commerce would shut down. It would take us back to the Stone Age where we would have to barter or trade in commodities instead of using a currency. How could we accept a credit card payment if the bank into which we deposit it might be bankrupt tomorrow and not pay us? How could we pay our vendors if the checks we send them with sufficient funds in our account are not honored because the bank went out of business?

This was all unthinkable. We went about our daily lives with these basic assumptions. I held all kinds of insurance including health, disability, liability, fire, windstorm, flood, and more. I invest funds conservatively and hedge currency and market risks. What I never considered was the risk of AIG going out of business and the insurance policies they were underwriting being worthless. AIG was one of the highest-rated insurance companies. Who would think that the world's major rating companies – including Moody's and Standard and Poor's – could be wrong?

But despite all these assumptions, the impossible happened. Lehman Brothers went bankrupt. Merrill Lynch, Citibank, AIG, and most other financial institutions were about to fail. Goldman Sachs had to be bailed out by Warren Buffett.

The world was in shock. The world economy was on the brink of shutting down. Even the savviest investors saw their net worth plummeting in value.

As I sat back and thought about what was going on, I realized that the solid ground we walk on is an illusion. As a student of the Bible for twelve years in a yeshiva, I knew that everything we have is a gift that can be taken away any time.

With rising wealth and success, did we lose focus on what is really important? Did we wake up every morning being thankful for our health, family, friends, and wealth? Did we think about the consequences if any of these should be taken away from us? Did we think for a moment that what we have can't be taken away? We work so hard our whole lives for wealth, we place such importance on it, and we assume it will always be there. But God can take it away anytime. And when He does, what do we have left?

When the markets were crashing, after a period of watching CNBC nonstop, I decided to turn it off. I stopped reading every article in the *Wall Street Journal* and *Barron's*. I stopped listening to commentators trying to explain what was going on. As a student of the Bible, I recognized what was going on. As I watched the total panic on Treasury Secretary Hank Paulson's face during television interviews, I realized that God had stepped in. Modern portfolio theory no longer applied. Diversification didn't matter. All asset classes were declining quickly. God was testing us. Was wealth all that mattered? Weren't our health and families important? What had we accomplished, other than the accumulation of wealth that might no longer exist? I did my best to secure my portfolio and realized that it was time to focus on my real mission. Was I accomplishing it?

Sometimes we need to be woken up and reminded that we were given tools for a purpose. Until they are taken away, we don't appreciate them. Are we using them for the purpose intended?

If it takes such hard work to earn wealth, and so little time for it to evaporate, why do we focus almost all our energy on wealth accumulation? The Bible does not discourage us from accumulating wealth, provided we use this wealth also for *tikkun olam* (repair of the world), to improve the world around us, giving a minimum of 10 percent to charity. (If we have sufficient wealth, that percentage should be higher.) This is a small percentage; we pay more than that in US taxes. This is God's take for giving us this wealth. God doesn't employ IRS auditors and examiners to question whether we paid our 10 percent (or more), but He knows what we have done with our wealth. If we have used it only for our own enjoyment, we have not been proper stewards of these assets. And remember, funds may be in our account, but they don't truly belong to us; they belong to our Creator. We only have money temporarily. It can be taken away anytime, as we witnessed in September 2008. Our wealth is an illusion. Use it the right way. Earn it the right way.

From a biblical perspective, wealth is just one tool we have been given. Sometimes we need to be woken up and reminded that we were given tools for a purpose. Until they are taken away, we don't appreciate them. Are we using them for the purpose intended?

The Great Recession made me even more focused on my life's goals. I asked myself some serious questions and I suggest you do the same.

1. Am I leading an ethical life?

Are we honest in our business dealings? We spend so much of our time at work. What if all the funds we saved from years of working were wiped out? Could we look back and say that all that time was productive? Was there more to our jobs and businesses than the funds we saved? Did we use our positions to encourage people around us to be charitable? Did we encourage charitable giving in our organizations? Did we create an environment of honesty and integrity? Did we pay our workers on time and fairly? Were we honest to our customers and our partners? When faced with difficult questions, did we choose the ethical route, even though it might not be the most profitable one? In short, have we left a legacy of decency?

2. Am I fulfilling my mission in life?

What have we done to improve our world? What people and organizations have we helped? Have we given at least 10 percent of our income to charity? Have we used our talents to improve the world around us? Have we dedicated our time to improving our people and community? Will we leave this earth in better shape than when we arrived?

3. Am I perpetuating my values?

Are we raising families and making sure that the values and principles we hold most dear will continue? If we don't have children of our own, or they are grown, are we making sure that our communities have the resources to teach the continuity of our values and principles? Do we lead a life worthy of emulating? Are we teaching our children or young people in our communities what is important to us? Are we motivating them?

After the 2008 recession, I doubled down on teaching my kids. I have prepared four of my kids for their bar/bat mitzvahs. I studied Bible with my oldest son almost every night for years. I now study Bible with my younger son almost nightly. I have had no greater pleasure than studying with my kids. The Great Recession brought me much closer to my children.

With the perspective I gleaned from studying the Bible, the recession of 2008 became a great opportunity to focus on my mission and purpose in life. We should all do the same introspection and have the same perspective during any tough economic period.

A Dozen Ways of Taking Inventory

If you lost all your money, what would be left?
A period of economic loss can be an opportunity to
strip away the superficialities of our lives and see the core.
Here are some questions to ask yourself
about the things that really matter.

1. Am I leading an ethical life?
   Am I honest in my business dealings?

2. What if all the funds I saved from years of working
   were wiped out? Could I look back and say
   that all that time was productive?

3. Have I given at least 10 percent of my income to charity?

4. Am I using the talents my Creator gave me effectively?

5. Am I fulfilling my mission in life?

6. Am I doing enough toward that mission?

7. Have I done something today
   to make the world a better place?

8. What people or organizations have I helped?

9. Do I lead a life worth emulating?

10. Am I raising a family and making sure that the values
    and principles I hold most dear will continue?

11. If I don't have my own children, or they are already grown,
    am I making sure that my community has the resources
    to teach the continuity of my values and principles?

12. Will I leave this earth in better shape than when I arrived?

16
Give Back

The generous soul shall be made rich, and he who satisfies abundantly shall be satisfied also himself.
– Proverbs 11:25

The Bible teaches us not only how to build a successful business, but also what to do once it is successful. The Bible teaches us to be socially responsible and not forget about those who don't have food, clothing, and shelter. Once we have established successful businesses, we have a social responsibility to our communities. We are obligated to donate a portion of our profits to the needy. Encourage your employees, partners, and customers to also be charitable through incentive programs, matching programs, and community service. Donate a portion of your profits to charity. Run promotions that contribute a portion of every sale to a worthy cause. Use your business as a vehicle for community improvement. We learn from Proverbs 11:25 that being charitable will make our businesses even more successful. Be generous with charity and you will be rewarded with even more success.

Once we have established successful businesses, we have a social responsibility to our communities.

Following are some specific strategies for charitable giving through your business.

1. Donate a portion of your profits to charity.

Promise to donate at least 10–20 percent of your profits annually to charity. The more you earn, the more you have to give away. Help the needy with the first 10–20 percent of your income, and you take home the bulk of the profit. Your business now has a meaningful purpose. Whenever you make a profit, you are also helping the needy. You will work harder because you know you are doing great things with a portion of the profit.

The Bible teaches us that earning money for no purpose other than the pursuit of profit is vanity. "He who loves money will not be satisfied with money, nor he who loves abundance with his income; this also is vanity" (Ecclesiastes 5:9[1]). The great King Solomon taught us that money in and of itself has no value. "There is a grievous evil that I have seen under the sun: namely, riches kept by their owner to his hurt, and those riches were lost in a bad venture, and if he has a son, there is nothing in his hand" (Ecclesiastes 5:12–13[2]). Money can be lost anytime. While you are earning it, make your business more meaningful by helping others with a portion of the profits.

Many big companies are now doing this and setting a great example for all of us. Kroger donates 10.9 percent of profits

---

1.   In Christian Bibles this verse is numbered 5:10.
2.   In Christian Bibles these verses are numbered 13–14.

annually to charity. It funds programs to feed the hungry and allows the Salvation Army to have people at its stores to collect funds. Macy's donates 8.1 percent of its profits to charity. It sponsors the annual Thanksgiving Day Parade in New York City and funds many local community projects. Safeway donates 7.5 percent of its profits to charities including Easter Seals, Special Olympics, Muscular Dystrophy Association, prostate cancer and breast cancer initiatives. Walmart donates over $300 million annually to charities focusing on hunger and community development. Goldman Sachs, Bank of America, and Exxon each donate more than $200 million annually to charity. Morgan Stanley donates 5.7 percent of its profits to charity. Target donates 5 percent of its profits to charity amounting to over $150 million per year.

These are just some examples of the many companies donating a portion of their income to charity. Their customers appreciate what they do and are more loyal because of it. I encourage anyone with a business – regardless of the type of business or location – to take your business to a higher level and donate a portion of your profits to charity.

2. Donate a portion of your stock ownership to a charity or foundation.

This is a tax-efficient way to build a platform for charitable giving. You are entitled to a tax deduction for the fair market value of the gift you make to a charity or foundation. This deduction will offset your other income. In addition, you can sell highly appreciated stock after it is donated to the foundation without paying a capital gains tax on the sales. Our tax code is set up with this double benefit to encourage this kind of charitable giving. Every time I sold a portion of hotels.com, I first donated part of the stock to my foundation. With this stock and contributions from my income, I have built a great platform for charitable giving that continues in perpetuity. My main motivation for building getaroom.com is that it will enlarge my pool of annual charitable giving.

When you donate part of your stock to charity or a foundation, your employees, partners, and customers will appreciate what you do and will want to help you succeed. You will no longer be merely a selfless business person pursuing profit, but a biblical entrepreneur who has a higher goal – building a larger charitable pool to help others.

3. Encourage charitable giving by your employees.

You can encourage all of your employees to be charitable. Simply match their charitable giving. Thus, if your employees give $100 to the Salvation Army, a United Way campaign, or other charity, you give another $100 and it becomes $200. Your employees will be able to participate in more community charities with employer matching. Employees will highly value this company benefit, and you will become a role model for other businesses.

4. Start a Charity Day.

Set up a day for your employees to do community volunteer work. Although in the short term it may be a day of lost employee productivity, employees will be so appreciative of the work the company is doing for the community that they will likely be even more productive going forward and more than make up for this day. It is also great PR for your company: customers prefer to support companies that do good things. Some large companies have set up programs to encourage others to volunteer their time to charities. Disney and HandsOn Network launched "Give a Day, Get a Disney Day," where they offered a free admission for a day at Disney when you volunteered a day to a charity. This program produced over a million volunteers in twelve weeks. Starbucks set up the "I'm In" program, which offered a free tall coffee for anyone who volunteered five or more hours to a charity. This produced over 1.2 million committed hours in just four days. Be creative in your business by setting up programs to encourage employee and customer community involvement.

5. Donate a portion of the purchase price of your products as a marketing promotion.

For every product bought, donate a percentage or fixed dollar amount to charity. Customers will want to purchase from you instead of the competition because part of their purchase price is going to a good cause. You create great marketing for your business and make your customers charitable.

6. Ask your customers to contribute at checkout.

There are hundreds of national and many local companies that raise funds for charities through checkout charity. They simply ask their customers if they want to add funds for a charity when they are checking out. Some of the well-known merchants doing this include Whole Foods, Costco, Kmart, JCPenney, eBay, Apple, Safeway, Publix, McDonald's, Chili's, and more. Programs range from asking for a dollar or two to offering pink ribbons or another item of recognition for sale. JCPenney raised over $10 million in six months just by asking customers to round their purchases to the next dollar. National campaigns like this raise over $358 million annually for charities. This is an easy way to raise significant funds for the causes of your choice.

7. Use business connections to make others charitable.

You will likely meet a lot of people through your business that you would not have otherwise met. When you tell them about the charity work you are involved in, many will want to help you. This is an opportunity to make others charitable and bring more supporters into the charities that you care about.

View your work as a means and not an end. When you follow biblical principles, you can build a great business and then give back. When we help others, we feel fulfilled and accomplished. When you leverage your business to improve the community around you, you wake up every day and appreciate what you have accomplished for the community.

There are many ways to give back. You can leverage your talents to help organizations that are helping the needy. You can spend time assessing how you can improve your community. You can donate to causes you believe in and encourage others to do so. The key is to remember that you need to complete the cycle that starts with following biblical principles to build your career and business. Reaching success in your business is not a final step; you are not done yet! You must now put just as much effort into using your success to help others and figuring out the most effective way to do that. You need to complete the circle of following biblical principles, earning the rewards from this, and then giving a portion of those rewards away to help others and improve your community. This is what I call the biblical cycle. Stopping at earning wealth is a big mistake. To be fulfilled in life, you must complete the biblical cycle. Giving back to your community is what it's all about.

17

Take Your Business
to a Higher Level

Our work is meaningless unless to do good.
– Ecclesiastes 3:12

n this book, I have shown you how to succeed by running
your business in an ethical way following biblical principles. There is more you can do to make your business
life much more meaningful. You can make your business a
platform for charitable giving by you, your employees, partners,
and customers. When your business operates not solely for profit,
but also to help others and make others charitable, you take your
business to a higher level and gain much more fulfillment from
your business career. This chapter brings examples of things we
and other companies have done to operate our businesses at a
higher level. By making your business a platform for charitable
giving, and focusing not just on profit but on operating ethically
and helping others, you become a biblical entrepreneur. You
seek profit, but your main motivation is helping others. Every

business owner can become a biblical entrepreneur and make his or her business life more meaningful.

Enact policies for direct and indirect charitable giving (see previous chapter for detailed suggestions). Give of your resources and use your business as a vehicle to encourage your employees, customers, and business associates to be charitable as well.

Every business owner can become a biblical entrepreneur and make his or her business life more meaningful.

Volunteer your skills and services to charities that need your help. Use your skills to help the charities that are important to you to succeed. Your time and expertise can often be even more valuable than donating funds.

Build your business on ethical principles and treat customers properly. As a biblical entrepreneur, you run your business honestly. You disclose material facts to your customers and never do a deal that is not honest.

Tell your customers and business partners when they make an honest mistake. People make honest mistakes all the time, such as double payments, paying a higher amount, shipping too many goods, etc. Your obligation is to notify the one making the honest mistake and return his or her money or goods.

Always keep your word, whether written or oral. Your integrity is more important than any increase in profit. Remember that "A good name is rather to be chosen than great riches, and esteem rather than silver or gold" (Proverbs 22:1).

Treat your employees, partners, and customers properly. Don't take undue advantage of your employees or those with whom you do business. Always treat them fairly, honestly, and above board.

Pay your employees on time.

Provide all goods and services as agreed.

Treat money entrusted to you as if it were your own. Treat deposits, funds given to you to invest, or money entrusted to you for any other purpose as your own.

Don't buy stolen goods. Don't buy products from companies that take advantage of their workers or that are dishonest. A biblical entrepreneur discourages this behavior and does not support companies like this.

When you run your business as a platform for your charitable activity and other biblical values, the time you spend at work becomes more productive and much more meaningful. Now you're answering to a higher authority. That's what being a biblical entrepreneur is all about.

Ten Ways to Operate Your Business on a Biblical Level

1. Give to charity and encourage your employees, customers, and associates to do so as well.

2. Volunteer your skills and services to charities and community organizations.

3. Never do a deal that is not honest.

4. Don't profit from other people's honest mistakes.

5. Always keep your word.

6. Treat your employees, partners, and customers fairly.

7. Pay your employees on time.

8. Provide all goods and services just as agreed.

9. Treat money entrusted to you as if it were your own.

10. Don't buy stolen goods or otherwise support companies that do not embody biblical values.

18

Sell Your Business Using Biblical Estate Planning

And you shall teach them diligently to your children.

– Deuteronomy 6:7

Assuming you followed the biblical principles in this book, your business has been successful and you are ready to sell or otherwise enter into a liquidity event for your business. You want to make sure that not only do you transfer your wealth to the next generation in a tax-efficient manner, but that you also transfer your values at the same time. You also now have a great opportunity to set up tax-efficient charitable planning. While I was getting ready to sell hotels.com, I spent a lot of time doing estate planning in three areas: multigenerational transfer of wealth, effective ways to transfer the values I cherished most as a guide for future generations, and setting up tax-efficient charitable giving so that my heirs will be engaged in charity in perpetuity, while also setting up a vehicle to do significant charitable giving during my lifetime.

You want to n[ot] only transfer your wealth to the next generation in a tax-efficient manner, but also transfer your values at the same time

Estate planning is planning for the transferring of your assets in the most tax-efficient manner and designating the recipients of your assets. I executed a legal will and set up multigenerational trusts. After spending months preparing my estate plan and completing the documents, I realized that I was missing the most important part of estate planning. I had planned for the transferring of my physical assets but I hadn't yet planned for the transferring of my intangible assets: the values, lessons, and traditions that I wanted to pass on to my children.

Biblical estate planning is not only providing for the transfer of physical assets via a legal will but also providing for the transfer of the intangible assets that you want to pass on to future generations. The Bible sets forth the great tradition of passing ethical teachings on from one generation to another: "and you shall teach them diligently to your children" (Deuteronomy 6:7). I believe that the best way to ensure continuity of what is important to you is to teach your children, show them by example, and involve them in your philanthropy and community work. But how do you continue this when you are no longer here? I found three effective ways to fulfill our obligation of continuity through biblical estate planning and ensure that our children and future generations receive our intangible value assets.

1. Incorporate your values in your estate documents.

We drafted our estate documents to incorporate and stress the importance of the values that we want to pass on: leading productive lives, getting married, raising a family, providing for a biblical education, travel to the Holy Land, and more. By both specifying the importance of these values and providing incentives to follow them, we help ensure that they will be passed on to future generations. For example, we provided for funding of trips to Israel, private religious school education, and other educational programming. We provided for matching funds for productive income generation and incentives to getting married and starting a family. When our children and future generations read our documents, they will understand how important these were to us. By providing economic incentives for the activities we believe in most strongly, we encourage future generations to pursue these as well.

2. Provide for sustained family giving.

I wanted to ensure that my children and future generations will continue to be involved in giving charity. I did this by setting up a foundation and donating company stock and income into the foundation. Through these gifts, we have built up substantial assets in our foundation over time and it is now our family vehicle for charitable giving. It is also part of our biblical estate planning, since the foundation is set up in perpetuity and it will ensure that my children and future generations of my family will be charitable.

The foundation must pay out at least 5 percent of the principal every year, so as long as assets in the foundation are growing at faster than 5 percent, the value of the foundation continues to grow. The foundation will ensure that my descendants will be charitable for multiple generations. Since long-term equity growth including dividend reinvestment and the impact of compounding have historically been and are projected to remain higher than the annual required distribution rate, we expect our foundation to last in perpetuity.

I set it up so that each of our children and future descendants will have the option of joining our foundation board. Each child also has the right to designate giving up to a certain portion of the annual giving. This way we planned to involve our descendants in charitable giving and allow them to be active in their local communities and to contribute to projects that are most meaningful to them.

We specified the categories of allowed giving and the maximum percentage of the annual grants allowed in each category. We also specified the type of organizations that the foundation may not issue grants to. In doing this, we leave enough flexibility for our descendants to be engaged in their communities and projects that they have an interest in but made sure that our foundation never issues grants to organizations that contradict our values.

Setting up your own foundation can be costly, and you don't have to do this. There are many donor-advised funds – such as Vanguard and Fidelity – run by major communities, charities, and firms that will manage these for you at minimal fees. They can typically be set up with as little as a few thousand dollars. You can add to the fund over time. These managed funds provide a tax-efficient way to consolidate, accrue, administer, and grant charitable gifts in perpetuity. They alleviate the administrative burdens and time required to invest assets, conduct due diligence, and issue grants.

3. Draft an ethical will.

In addition to executing a legal will, I executed an ethical will (see the next chapter) because I believe that passing on the values and lessons I have learned during my lifetime is much more important than any physical assets I can leave my children. Many of these values and lessons I learned from my parents and grandparents, and I am continuing the great tradition of passing these on to the next generation. As I have accumulated more assets, the intangibles have become more important to me and the tangibles less important. My ethical will is intended to enrich my descendants' lives and make them much more meaningful. I hope that future generations will look to it frequently for guidance, comfort, spiritual inspiration, and to help them put their lives in proper perspective.

Values, ideals, and lessons are too important to be left to chance, and are certainly no less important than material assets. Rather than merely passively hoping that your children and descendants will know what your values were and will carry them forward, take active steps to formally communicate your values to them through biblical estate planning.

The Three Pillars
of Biblical Estate Planning

1. Incorporate your values in your estate documents.
2. Provide for sustained family giving.
3. Draft an ethical will.

Perpetuate Your Values through an Ethical Will

Children of Jacob,
come and listen to your father Israel....
– Genesis 49:2

The concept of an ethical will is itself a biblical idea. In Genesis 49, Jacob gathers his children together to sum up his final teachings and blessings to them before he dies. Moses, too, gathers the people together to hear his parting words of wisdom in the book of Deuteronomy. "And when Moses finished speaking all these words to all Israel, he said to them, 'Pay attention to all the words I testify to you this day, that you may charge your children to observe to do all the words of this law'" (Deuteronomy 32:45–46). Since antiquity, there has been a practice of setting down final thoughts and teachings in an ethical will and more recently in legacy letters.

It's never too early to consider the legacy you will one day leave in the world. A great way to focus your life is to craft an ethical will in which you lay out for yourself in a concrete fashion the lessons and values that you'd like to leave behind for those who will come after you. An ethical will or legacy letter is a priceless document to leave to your loved ones to help them carry your values forward into the next generation. But even more than that, identifying what you will want to be remembered for someday can actually help you to shape and create your life today.

In this chapter I'll share with you some of the items that I included in my ethical will. I offer these merely as a guideline for others who also want to draft an ethical will. We are all unique and have learned lessons that we want to pass on in different ways. What is important is to set out how you learned these values and why they are important to you. My ethical will also specifies the formative events and people in my life that influenced who I am:

> ⇨ **Twelve years in a Jewish day school:** Twelve years of studying Bible and Prophets gave me a great understanding and appreciation for the sacred texts and formed the value system I live by today.

> ⇨ **Growing up in a household with strong biblical values:** Growing up in a home following the Bible and celebrating the Sabbath and holidays as a family showed me the value and importance of tradition in keeping the family together.

⇨ **My parents:** My father constantly encouraged me to practice rituals and expand my knowledge by reading and studying more. Working for my father and going with him on sales calls helped me develop my marketing and sales skills. My mother taught me to always be courteous and to have a positive attitude.

⇨ **My grandparents:** My maternal grandmother taught me that differences of opinion in a relationship should be discussed amicably and never end up in an argument. My maternal grandfather taught me that there is nothing more important than integrity and being honest. My paternal grandmother taught me the importance of keeping traditions. My paternal grandfather taught me the importance of charity and community involvement.

⇨ **Summers in Israel:** I learned just how rich people's lives can be without materialism.

⇨ **Talmud study:** I developed much of my analytical skills through my Talmudic study. This prepared me for the rigorous analytical work in law school and practice; I use these skills daily to analyze issues.

⇨ **Higher education:** Many of the skills I still use today I learned from college, law school, and law practice. There is no substitute for developing decision-making, communication, and other skills needed for life.

⇨ **Community leadership:** My leadership positions in local and national organizations have made my life so much more meaningful. I have met some of my best friends and many great leaders through this volunteer work.

⇨ **My spouse and children:** There is no greater gift than your spouse and children. The more love and attention I give them, the more I get back.

The second section of my ethical will sets out important life lessons and ethical teachings that I have internalized in my lifetime and that I'd like my children and theirs to continue to practice. Following are some examples of the items I included in my ethical will. We are all unique and have values we cherish most and want to pass on to the next generation. Write your own ethical will. I hope this list will be a guide and give you ideas for the kind of teachings you want to include in your own ethical will.

Integrity

- **Be honest in business dealings.** It is much more important to be honest in a transaction than to earn a higher profit. There will always be opportunities for more profits, but once you are dishonest in a transaction this cannot be changed. It will affect your future dealings, for others will have less respect and trust in you. You will get great inner fulfillment from turning down a transaction that is not ethical.

- **Treat all human beings with dignity.** Regardless of the social status of a person, we were all created in God's image and you should treat all of your workers, associates, and others with the same measure of dignity.

- **Never state a fact that you are not 100 percent sure of.** It never hurts to say that you do not know the answer.

- **Never talk about others in a negative way.** Either remain silent or talk positively. There is no benefit to speaking badly about a person regardless of the circumstances, unless you are warning someone of imminent harm. If you hear evil talk of others, do not listen to it.

- **Be up-front with others and speak honestly.** It is much better to be up-front about issues than to cause someone to feel misled.

- **Never allow an injustice to occur.**

- **Your word is everything and more important than a written contract.** If you agree to something orally, fulfill your commitment.

- **Your heart and mouth should be the same.** Do not speak one way and think another. Be sincere.

- **Feed animals before you feed yourself.** They cannot feed themselves. Be kind to animals – they are God's creation.

- **When you hire others to do work, pay them on time.** Many people need to be paid on time to buy food for their families.

- **Taking time from your employer is stealing – be honest about time worked.**

- **Do not vote on issues where you are at all compromised.** Do not accept gifts when others are trying to change your vote.

- **Stay away from evil temptations.**

- **Be accountable and have the institutions that you are involved with be accountable.** Make sure they run efficiently.

- **Do not waste.** Our resources are limited and there is so much good to be done. Do not be wasteful.

- **Work hard.** There is no substitute in this world for hard work. Be a productive member of society. You will do well by being thorough, working hard, and making decisions based on analyzing all of the facts.

Tradition

- **Have a family.** People cannot reach their full potential alone. There is a right mate for you – life is so much more meaningful when you share it with someone you love. There are always risks, but they are risks worth taking. With a spouse you are never alone and always have someone you can count on. You can have children and become part of a community.

- **Become an active part of a community.** This is important, as it adds strength to everything you do.

- **Cherish your faith and traditions – this will tremendously enhance your life.** Make sure your community and religious institutions remain strong – especially religious schools.

- **Learn about your people and heritage.** The more you learn, the more you will appreciate your heritage.

- **Keep and cherish your traditions.** Attend synagogue or church. We have been blessed with a day of rest – the Sabbath. This is a great opportunity to renew ourselves, look back on the week, and see how we can improve the next week. It is an opportunity to soul-search and spend time with the family. Spend every Sabbath/Sunday/holiday together as a family – your children will look forward to these special days and it will strengthen your family life. Bless your children. Your life will be much more fulfilled when you say the prayers with meals and observe your other rituals.

- **Protect the State of Israel.** The words and prophesies of the Bible are now coming true and to life. It is up to you to do everything in your power to keep it strong as the nation of the Jewish people.

Relationships

- **As the great biblical scholar Hillel taught, the essence of the Bible is treating others properly.** Hillel taught: "What is hateful to you, do not do to others" (Babylonian Talmud, *Shabbat* 31a). I have learned that when you treat others well, you in turn will be treated well. You will also feel better about yourself, your career and business will improve, and you will have many more friends.

- **Take care of each other.** Stress the importance of having a great relationship with your siblings and looking out for each other, especially in time of need.

- **Perform deeds of kindness.** The secret to happiness and fulfillment is doing good deeds for others. There is no greater inner fulfillment than being able to help another person. The secondary benefit is that the person you help will look to help you in return. I suggest that

each and every day you do an act of kindness – you will be much more effective in everything else that you are doing because you will be glowing with the fulfillment from the good deed.

- **Develop a close relationship with someone you can always bounce ideas off and in whom you can confide.** I was very fortunate to have a business partner since law school, Dave Litman, whom I could always rely on and call to discuss issues. It is always better to discuss a plan with someone and get feedback before acting alone. Listen to others and let others criticize your work. Do not assume you are always right. Sometimes it is difficult to see the other side of an issue until someone else articulates it.

- **In looking for a spouse, look for a good heart.** Look for someone who cares about other people, who is empathetic and honest. Look for someone you can respect and grow together with. Look for someone you can always rely on.

- **Visit the sick.** Be there for friends and family in times of sorrow.

- **Attend your friends' and family's major events.** It means so much to people when you share their happy occasions. There is no substitute for being there for a major event in a friend's or family member's life.

- **Never hurt a person with words – this can often be more painful than physical damage.** In a relationship, be very careful what you say. Don't let emotion overcome reason.

- **Make your spouse happy and your spouse will make you happy.** Life involves compromise. Be accepting of the other person's personality and remember that marriage is a long-term commitment – think about what you are going to say

before you say it and be careful not to say anything bad regardless of how upset you may be. Be forgiving and understanding. Do not let minor issues be bothersome. Always be loyal and honest to your spouse in every way. Always be open.

- **Your family and friends come first.** Remember this when deciding on priorities. Teach and spend quality time with each of your kids. You can never make up lost time with your children. Always stay balanced in your life. Your life will be much more fulfilling when you find the right balance between family, friends, career, community, charity, and other things that are important to you.

- **When you fail to win an argument or negotiation, always leave the opponent with positive thoughts and an opening for further discussion.** Never end on bad terms. Always have closure – even though the relationship or transaction did not go the way you wanted. In the long run you are much better off to have closure and to end on good terms.

- **Share – with your family, friends, and community.** Share your feelings, sorrows, concerns. You are much stronger as part of a community.

- **Develop real relationships and friends.** A true friend is someone who deeply cares about you, and about whom you care in return. A true friend understands when you say no to something you believe is wrong.

- **Take an interest in other people.** When you show that you care, you will

develop great friends. Go out of your way to help your friends and the friendships will grow even greater.

- **Always be courteous.** Regardless of how disrespectful your opponent is, or how upset you are, always keep your decorum and remain respectful. Respect for you will grow greatly when people know you are always respectful.

- **Remember that God alone can forgive you for sins against Him, but when you sin against another person, you must seek forgiveness first from that person.** If you do something wrong to someone, you need to go back and make it right.

Values and Attitude

- **Be modest.** Modesty is a great value. Be careful not to get pulled into being pompous. Those who act pompously are typically unhappy in their lives. People have much more

respect for a modest person, and you will feel much better about yourself when you act with humility.

- **Be merciful.** Have pity on others and be forgiving.

Holding grudges and being angry at others for long periods of time has no fulfillment. When you forgive and reestablish relationships, they can become much stronger, and you will be much more fulfilled than by holding a grudge. There is much inner strength earned by being able to forgive.

- **Be charitable.** The pursuit of capital and wealth for its own sake has no meaning. The pursuit of wealth to help others makes it worthwhile and meaningful. Spend as much time earning wealth as you do figuring out how and whom you are going to help with that wealth. Learn about causes you care about. Help not only by giving funds, but by giving ideas and becoming involved in improving the charities. Encourage others to become charitable. They will feel better about themselves by helping others. Remember that according to the great sage Maimonides, the highest form of charity is helping others become self-sufficient so they no longer need charity.

- **Put in your best effort in everything you do.** There is no excuse for not giving your all. You may not succeed every time, but you will succeed much more often when you give it your best.

- **Find something you love and become passionate about it.** You may not be the best at everything but work hard to be the best at what is important to you.

- **Success comes with hard work, dedication, being relentless, and believing in yourself.** There is no substitute for hard work. When you believe in something, it is much more likely to happen.

- **Be a productive member of society.** Find a career that allows you to support a family and that benefits others.

- **Be thorough.** Make decisions based on analyzing all of the facts. Do not guess. Act through knowledge.

- **Establish goals.** Work is much more exciting and achievable when you are working toward a defined goal.

- **Follow your instincts.** If you have doubts, listen to them and always double-check before acting. Your instincts are often correct.

- **Do your homework.** Before you take a position or negotiate a transaction, research it thoroughly. There is no excuse for being unprepared or unaware of publicly available facts.

- **Be persistent when you believe in a cause.** I have championed many causes when the majority did not agree with me, but I was persistent whenever I believed that I was right. When you believe the cause is right and just, then do not give up.

- **Be a leader, not a follower.** Each of you knows right from wrong. Don't be tempted by peer pressure.

- **You are here on Earth for a reason.** Before you do something that may be wrong, think about how you will look at this twenty or thirty years later. Make every day meaningful. Live a holy and spiritual life. You will look back later in life and cherish the good deeds you have done. All you have is time. Make it meaningful.

- **Be positive about life.** It is always better to see the glass half full instead of half empty. My business career was mostly about marketing. When you are positive and upbeat and optimistic, others will flock to you or your products.

- **Be thankful.** Every day, be thankful that you are where you are. A wealthy person is one who is satisfied with what he or she has. This is true wealth. Appreciate that we can walk, talk, see, and so on. Do not take things for granted.

Although an ethical will is a great way to record and transmit your values to future generations, the best way to teach these values to your loved ones is to practice them yourself during your lifetime. I find that the most effective way to teach is by example. Your ethical will reinforces the values you have lived by and thereby taught your children during your lifetime.

There's no question that someday your written record of your life's lessons will be of tremendous value to those you will leave behind. But you can start enjoying the tangible benefits of writing an ethical will immediately: the very act of sitting down to record for posterity what is most important to you in life will focus you on your life's mission and clarify your values right here and now. Also, consider reviewing your ethical will annually and making any appropriate updates.

Don't wait. Write an ethical will or legacy letter today.

Eight Things to Include in an Ethical Will

1. The values that are most important to you and that you want your family to continue

2. Why these values are so important to you

3. The people who have influenced your life the most

4. The events that have influenced your life the most

5. Advice for success

6. Family traditions

7. Advice on relationships

8. How to get the most out of life

Afterword

The Talmudic Formula for Success and Balance in Life

You shall not stop talking about the Bible, but rather meditate on it day and night, so that you may be careful to act according to all that is written therein; for then you will be prosperous, and then you will be successful.
– Joshua 1:8

This book has been about how to achieve business success by following the ethical principals in the Bible. But what about success overall in life? How do you achieve the right balance of family, study, work, and community?

My first job out of law school was practicing corporate and securities law at Gibson, Dunn & Crutcher, one of the largest law firms in the world. After practicing law there for a couple of years, I decided to pursue my entrepreneurial passions and start a travel business. I wrote earlier about many of the lessons I learned from my first company. I worked hard and had a passion to succeed. My dream was to have enough annual profits to sell the company and have enough funds from the sale to retire and do whatever I wanted to do for the rest of my life. Buy a nice condo, fancy sports car, travel, and more. When we exceeded that annual profit goal, I sold the company and moved back to Florida, where I grew up, to enjoy life. I thought I had reached a level of great success, but six months later I was so bored, I didn't feel successful. I felt a lot was missing.

During those few months, and before I started my next career in the hotel business, I started looking for answers to why I didn't feel fulfilled. I remembered learning from my paternal grandfather, Juda Diener, that the best place to search for answers to life's tough questions is the Talmud. I watched him study Talmud almost every day. The Talmud is an explanation of the Bible. It was written between the years 200 and 500 CE. It consists of sixty-three sections and is several thousand pages long. It is written in a language called Aramaic and contains the teachings of thousands of rabbinical scholars on the explanation of the Bible, religious law, civil law, ethics, philosophy, lore, and more. It is the basis of Jewish law.

As a witness to the Holocaust, my grandfather believed the way to win the war against those determined to destroy the Jewish people is to educate our people on our great traditions and sacred texts. Only when we understand and appreciate the great heritage and resources we have will we fight to preserve them. He gave away a large portion of his earnings to start and maintain Jewish day schools. He believed that the Talmud was the backbone of Judaism and that if he could get thousands of people studying Talmud regularly, it would make them much more committed to preserving Judaism. My grandfather, together with Rabbi Pinchas Teitz, one of the top leaders and scholars at the time, came up with the brilliant idea back in the fifties of broadcasting a page of Talmud every week on New York radio. There was no Internet then; the major place people went for news was the radio. This program was so successful that it lasted for thirty-six years.

I spent many years in Jewish day school learning the Talmud and the Aramaic language and was always impressed at the great wisdom of its teachings. Many of my law school cases were almost the same cases I had studied in the Talmud. I believe the reason I was at the top of my law school class at Cornell was that I had studied and analyzed many of the classic cases for years before I arrived. I had already studied the analytical methods used in law school learning Talmud. My Talmud teachers used the same Socratic method of teaching that my law professors used. For me, law school was just a continuation of my Talmudic study. Many of the business concepts in this book came from lessons I learned in the Talmud as well.

I knew the Talmud was also the right place to figure out what I was missing after I sold my first business.

Had I really achieved success? Webster's dictionary defines success as "the fact of getting or achieving wealth, respect, or fame." What was the Talmud's definition for success?

I found Judaism's formula for success in life in the tractate of *Shabbat* 31a mentioned in earlier chapters. It is a rabbinical discussion of the questions one is asked at the end of one's days in the heavenly court. The scholars discuss the ultimate questions asked as a way of explaining what is most important in life and to determine how one can measure the success of one's life.

Here are the main questions asked:

> The questions one is asked in the heavenly court at the end of one's days are a way of explaining what is most important in life and measuring the success of one's life.

1. Were you honest in your business dealings?

The first question we are asked is whether or not we were honest in business. The Bible places an emphasis on one's character and teaches that the most important thing one can do in life is to be honest, especially when the temptation is to do the opposite. It is not achieving wealth but *how* that wealth is obtained that defines success. If it is obtained dishonestly, it is valueless. The Bible measures success in life by asking whether we keep our promises, whether we have personal integrity and put honesty above profit. The true measure of success in life is integrity.

2. Did you set aside regular time to study?

Without regular study, we lose focus and often go down the wrong path. With regular study, we can continue to improve and utilize the brain and talents our Creator has given us to the fullest. We need to constantly evaluate where we are in life and strive to improve. At the end of life we'll be held accountable: Did you strive to improve, or were you satisfied with the status quo? Did you implement the things you learned?

After studying this piece of Talmud, I started devoting one hour every week to study. I closed my door and studied for an hour with either a Talmudic scholar or study group. I since expanded this to almost daily study with my kids. I'm amazed how much more fulfilled I am after an hour of study. But we need to make it a priority and do it regularly, regardless of how busy we are. We can only grow ourselves and improve with study. We can only follow the Bible if we understand it. Don't say to yourself that you don't have the time: spending time studying the Bible will actually energize you to use the rest of your time more productively. We feel more comfortable spending more time in our business when we have fulfillment coming from our study.

3. Did you build a family and support the education of the next generation?

Success is not just what we have done personally, but what we have done to pass on biblical values and wisdom to the next generation. Did you have children and raise them to continue the mission of improving the world around us? Whether you had your own children or not, did you make sure your community has the resources to provide a biblical education for the children in your community?

When I reevaluated my life and began searching for meaning, I decided it was time to get serious about finding a mate and raising a family. I changed my whole approach toward dating and stopped wasting time dating anyone who didn't share my values. I looked for a spouse who wanted a large family, a home following biblical principles, who understood the importance of a biblical education and wanted to be involved in the community. I looked for a spouse who had the qualities I wanted to pass on to my children: honesty, integrity, warmth, empathy, humility, humor, a concern for others, and more.

4. Did you do your part to improve the world around you and make it better than when you arrived?

When you look back at your life, what will you be able to say you contributed to make the world around you better? Success is not just achieving wealth but how we use that wealth. Did we use it only for ourselves, or did we use it to help others and improve our communities? I try to take this seriously. I was not fulfilled by my pursuit and accumulation of wealth in and of itself. Something was missing. When we have wealth, we become a steward of that wealth. It is just as difficult to find the right places to give our wealth as it is to earn the wealth. But fulfillment and success only comes from the complete package. Earning it without spending it right is not success. Earning it and working hard to find the best use of that wealth is how we become truly successful. I decided to make sure I did something every day to improve our world. I set up my foundation and regularly donated a portion of my income. I became involved in the community. I found the organizations I believed were making the biggest impact on improving our local community, backing the State of Israel, maintaining US support of Israel, educating our children, promoting biblical values, helping children with special needs, and providing for the needy. I actively volunteered my time to help make those organizations more efficient with the business skills I had. I encouraged and recruited others to give and become active.

These questions have become my guiding light. Why not ask yourself these questions now and make sure you will have the right answers when you get to the heavenly court?

Ready for the Heavenly Court

These are the questions you will be asked
when you finish your days on this earth.
When the time comes,
how successful will you be able to call your life?

1. Were you honest in your business dealings?. . . . . . . ☐

2. Did you set aside regular time to study?. . . . . ☐

3. Did you build a family and support the
education of the next generation?. . . . . ☐

4. Did you do your part to improve
the world around you and make it
better than when you arrived?. . . . . ☐

About the Author

BOB DIENER is the cofounder of the company that became hotels.com and the president and co-founder of getaroom.com, which was named the best hotel booking site by frommers.com. After receiving his law degree from Cornell, where he was an editor of the *Law Review*, Bob practiced securities and corporate law with the law firm of Gibson, Dunn & Crutcher. Along with his partner, David Litman, he created the merchant model for booking hotel rooms and launched one of the first travel sites on the web. They sold a majority interest in the company to Interactive Corp. and took the company public as CEO and president in early 2000. Their stock price soared from $16 to over $90 in one of the most successful IPOs ever.

As a leading travel industry expert, Bob is a frequent source for many major news organizations, as well as a recurrent guest on many television and radio stations including NBC, CNN, and Fox News. Bob is featured on KGO Radio in San Francisco every Sunday morning, and his articles have been published on sites such as Aish.com and in journals such as the *Harvard Business Review*.

Bob has taught business practice at the Cornell Law School and has been a scholar in residence at the University of Florida Entrepreneurship program. He was recently named the Alumni Entrepreneur of the Year by the University of Florida. Bob lives with his family in Miami, where he is an avid triathlete.

Work Hard to Succeed

Do Your Homework

Use Your Talents

Determine Your Value Proposition

Hire – and Keep – the Right Employees

Limit Risk

Be Frugal and Minimize Debt

Find Solutions

Be Humble: Accept and Encourage Criticism

Have the Highest Level of Customer Service

Be Transparent with Customers

Take the High Road

Build a Reputation for Integrity

Obey the Law

Prepare for Difficult Economic Times

Give Back

Take Your Business to a Higher Level

Sell Your Business Using Biblical Estate Planning

Perpetuate Your Values through an Ethical Will

Made in the USA
San Bernardino, CA
31 October 2016